PREPAREDU

PREPAREDU

HOW INNOVATIVE COLLEGES DRIVE STUDENT SUCCESS

Gloria Cordes Larson, Esq.

President, Bentley University

Foreword by *Rosabeth Moss Kanter*

JB JOSSEY-BASS™
A Wiley Brand

Published by Jossey-Bass
A Wiley Brand
One Montgomery Street, Suite 1000, San Francisco, CA 94104-4594—www.josseybass.com

Jossey-Bass books and products are available through most bookstores. To contact Jossey-Bass directly call our Customer Care Department within the U.S. at 800-956-7739, outside the U.S. at 317-572-3986, or fax 317-572-4002.

Wiley publishes in a variety of print and electronic formats and by print-on-demand. Some material included with standard print versions of this book may not be included in e-books or in print-on-demand. If this book refers to media such as a CD or DVD that is not included in the version you purchased, you may download this material at http://booksupport.wiley.com. For more information about Wiley products, visit www.wiley.com.

Library of Congress Cataloging-in-Publication Data Is Available

Hardback ISBN: 9781119402398
ePDF ISBN: 9781119402480
ePub ISBN: 9781119402473

Cover design by: Wiley
Cover image: © pikcha/Shutterstock
Author Photo: © Taslim Sidi

Printed in the United States of America
FIRST EDITION

HB Printing   10 9 8 7 6 5 4 3 2 1

For the Bentley community – the hearts and minds behind PreparedU.

CONTENTS

ABOUT THE AUTHOR

GLORIA CORDES LARSON, ESQ., WAS ELECTED TO THE PRESIDENCY of Bentley University after a prestigious career as an attorney, public policy expert, and business leader. She was drawn to Bentley because of its inventive approach to redefining business education—by fusing its core business curriculum with the arts and sciences—and its strong focus on ethics and social responsibility.

During her tenure, the institution has reached a number of milestones centered around the content and value of a business education in the twenty-first-century marketplace. President Larson also launched the Center for Women and Business at Bentley in 2011, with a mission to advance shared leadership among women and men in the corporate world and to develop women as business leaders. Currently, she serves on the boards of directors of two public companies, Unum Group and Boston Private, as well as a number of nonprofit boards.

Before joining Bentley, Larson was co-chair of the Government Strategies Group at Foley Hoag LLP. She led a business advisory cabinet for Massachusetts Democratic governor Deval Patrick and served as secretary of economic affairs under Massachusetts Republican governor William Weld. Larson also oversaw business and regulatory issues as deputy director of consumer protection at the Federal Trade Commission in Washington DC.

President Larson has been named among *Boston* magazine's 50 Most Powerful People in 2015, the *Boston Business Journal's* Power 50: Influential Bostonians, and *Boston* magazine's 50 Most Powerful Women in Boston. She is the recipient of the International Women's Forum's Women Who Make a Difference Award (2015) and the Associated Industries of Massachusetts's Next Century Award (2015), as well as the Greater Boston Chamber of Commerce's inaugural Collaborative Leadership Award and Academy of Distinguished Bostonians Award.

BENTLEY UNIVERSITY is one of the nation's leading business schools, dedicated to preparing a new kind of business leader—one with the deep technical skills, broad global perspective, and high ethical standards required to make a difference in an ever-changing world. Our rich, diverse arts and sciences program, combined with an advanced business curriculum, prepares informed professionals who make an impact in their chosen fields. Located on a classic New England campus minutes from Boston, Bentley is a dynamic community of leaders, scholars, and creative thinkers. The graduate school emphasizes the impact of technology on business practice, in offerings that include MBA and master of science programs, PhD programs in accountancy and in business, and customized executive education programs. The university enrolls approximately forty-two hundred undergraduate students and a thousand graduate students. *Bloomberg BusinessWeek* ranks Bentley among the top ten undergraduate business programs in the country. The *Princeton Review's* annual best colleges guide names Bentley as number one in the nation for career services and internship opportunities. Bentley is accredited by the New England Association of Schools and Colleges; AACSB International—The Association to Advance Collegiate Schools of Business; and the European Quality Improvement System, which benchmarks quality in management and business education.

FOREWORD

SAVE THE PLANET, OR GET HIRED? DEVELOP DEEP EXPERTISE, or become a broad thinker? Be work-ready for today's jobs (based on yesterday's ideas), or create new ideas for the future?

Gloria Larson says you don't have to choose. You can have it all. Well, you can if only colleges and universities would finally "get it," and start connecting areas of knowledge and types of experience in powerful new ways.

A wise (and very successful) friend was responsible for commissioning young entrepreneurial talent to carry out Internet technology projects for his very old, very large company. At first, he issued requests complete with detailed specifications. The results were mediocre. Then he saw the flaw in his reasoning. In rapidly evolving fields, if he knew what to ask for, it was probably already obsolete. He needed not each company's last idea but its next idea. Instead of behaving like a teacher giving out assignments, he started turning the young tech firms into partners, cocreating new, cutting-edge solutions.

High-performance workplaces that seek constant innovation thrive on this kind of collaborative approach. So do Millennials entering the workforce in large numbers. I think of them in terms of my three Ms of motivation: mastery (stimulating challenges), membership (inclusion in the community), and meaning (a sense of purpose). The fourth M of money must be fair and sufficient, but often isn't the driver of great work.

To accomplish noble purposes such as reducing greenhouse gases or ending childhood hunger requires management blocking and tackling. To be successful financially requires thinking beyond the bottom line and understanding all the others who could block the business if not tackle the opportunity. The lines between fields in practice become barriers to overcome, getting in the way.

Entrepreneurs who create new ventures must be multifaceted and aware of their responsibilities to many constituencies beyond their immediate customers. Uber's founder started learning this when his ride-sharing company's growth as a technology platform was jeopardized by its failing to be responsible to stakeholders such as drivers (who felt they were more than independent contractors) or government officials (who felt antagonized by Uber's initial "rules don't apply to us" stance).

That's the point of the "hybrid learning" that Larson describes: connect important technical skills with the ability to think broadly and responsibly about the world via the liberal arts. Every business, nonprofit organization, and government agency I know is busily trying to get rid of "silos" in which homogeneous groups close ranks and talk only to one another. Why shouldn't the colleges and universities that educate future leaders help them become boundary crossers rather than sticking them in the silos of picking one major field or being on only one track? Companies are in trouble when manufacturing doesn't talk to marketing; communities have problems when the FBI has information not shared with local police. The Internet by itself doesn't erase the walls between groups or the borders between nations; that requires people who can build bridges. College—and maybe earlier education too—can lay the foundations for people who can speak many technical languages, relate to many diverse people, and know the importance of teamwork by experiencing it.

Larson has evidence that employers are coming to prefer people who have hybrid educations—technical and liberal arts. She argues that parents and prospective students should prefer this too, seeking places that cultivate that fusion. To make a sweeping generalization, the twentieth century was the age of specialized knowledge, when many fields became "professions" complete with their own certifications; the twenty-first century is the age of interdisciplinary knowledge, when the true skill is to find the connections, in order to tackle problems or build business opportunities that couldn't be handled by any one profession alone.

A college degree has long been essential; there is a significant disparity in life chances between those with and without a college degree. But college degrees, or even graduate degrees, haven't always been relevant to the work—or life—afterward. Sometimes getting a degree has been ticket punching to get in the door where the real learning begins. We can't afford that system any longer. College is too expensive; time is too precious. So colleges and universities must be held to the new standard of relevance.

Warren Bennis, a former university president and leadership guru, once said that a university is harder to change than a graveyard. An institution whose basic structure was laid down centuries ago in monasteries can be very hard to change. That's why it is exciting and heartening to see the experiments, reinventions, innovations, and soul-searching going on today in the quest to make higher education relevant to the work of this unfolding digital century. For that we can even think beyond Millennials and find ways to educate Boomers at late stages in their careers (financiers, lawyers, senior executives) in applying their capabilities to addressing major social and environmental problems, which is the premise behind the Harvard Advanced Leadership Initiative.

This book offers one university's story as a call to action to others. It shows how Bentley University, which originated as an accounting school and found fame through its emphasis on business ethics, has seized upon the marriage of liberal arts with professional management disciplines and the partnership of classroom and company experience. The goal is to better prepare students to be ready from day one to think creatively and collaboratively, advise decision makers, dream up improvements, move easily between for-profit and public or nonprofit sectors, and start small enterprises or change large ones.

This is also Gloria's story. (Note that she's on a first-name basis with all the students.) She provides illuminating glimpses of her own stellar journey across fields and sectors to have impact. But the understanding of many fields that took her almost a lifetime to accomplish—parents who are Baby Boomers will identify with that—now can be nurtured as part of the higher education process. This will produce graduates much better able to master challenges already visible as well as the ones sure to lie ahead.

Rosabeth Moss Kanter
Ernest L. Arbuckle Professor of Business Administration,
Harvard Business School

ACKNOWLEDGMENTS

LET ME START WHERE THE IDEA FOR THIS BOOK BEGAN, AND that's with David Perry, formerly chief marketing officer at Bentley University, and now chief marketing officer at University of Utah Health Sciences. Perry recognized early in our work together that Bentley's distinct integration of business and the arts and sciences, coupled with hands-on learning, technology, and career planning, was an especially powerful antidote to the pervasive perception among employers that today's college graduates are ill-prepared for the twenty-first-century workplace. The market research he commissioned validated Bentley's PreparedU approach to undergraduate business education, leading both of us to believe that ours was a story worth sharing with parents, students, business leaders, and educators. I will be forever grateful to Perry for his vision, creativity, and ever-present sense of humor—all of which inspired me to write this book.

I am also tremendously indebted to Doug Hardy, who spent the better part of two years bringing this book to life. His dedicated efforts included countless interviews with alumni, faculty, staff, employers, and others associated with Bentley and the additional schools featured; wide-ranging research that underpins many of the book's conclusions; and the seemingly endless rounds of drafting and editing that led to the "final" draft we ultimately handed off to the capable editors at Wiley. This is truly Doug's book as much as it is mine.

Thank you's go as well to Bentley's chief marketing officer, Val Fox, for seizing the opportunity to expand the book's reach and narrative, and to Chris Joyce, special advisor to the president, for his steely-eyed editing and many good suggestions around content. Both are talented writers in their own right, and this book is better for their significant efforts.

Perhaps my most obvious—and necessary—thanks go to the many outstanding teacher-scholars at Bentley. It is our faculty, after all, who are defining and delivering an exceptional business education on a daily basis—one that is designed to meet both current and future organizational and societal needs. The university's fusion of business and liberal arts is at the core of this unique model, and it is our faculty who most own the model and its resulting success for Bentley graduates.

I'm grateful as well to our school's dedicated student affairs professionals. They provide our students with a learning environment that both complements and extends the classroom experience, making student life an equal partner in a holistic Bentley education.

Thank you also to the now many thousands of Bentley students and alumni I've been privileged to know over the past decade. I reserve particular praise for the Millennial generation I got to know especially well. I continue to believe that Millennials are the most socially and globally conscious generation, inspiring me more every day to believe that the world will be better for their presence in it. Because of them, I chose to come to Bentley, and it's our students who have collectively helped make this the most rewarding chapter of my long career.

In addition to my Bentley colleagues, I thank and express my admiration for the higher education colleagues from other schools featured in this book, who are connecting the dots in smart, novel ways between what's taught in the classroom and the fast-paced, globalized world our graduates will enter. Many other additional educators across the country are doing so as well, recognizing that today's graduates need a different kind of college experience than previous generations, and it is gratifying to see so many colleges and universities rising to the occasion.

I reserve my last thank you's for my immediate family. Love and gratitude go to my husband, Allen, for supporting me in every way imaginable through many divergent career turns, including my late career foray into higher education. Always willing to lend a helping hand, he spent many hours over the 2016 Christmas holiday break reading an *almost* final draft of this book, asking thoughtful questions and offering the insightful suggestions that most often come from someone a step or two removed from the process. Love and gratitude go as well to our three English Labradors, Harry Jr., Sally, and Teak, who offered no critique whatsoever of PreparedU, opting instead for belly rubs and trips to the kitchen treat jar when they sensed I needed a break.

INTRODUCTION

IN FALL 2006, I TRAVELED FROM BOSTON TO CHARLOTTESVILLE, Virginia, to interview second-year law students at my alma mater, the University of Virginia School of Law (UVA). As a partner at the law firm Foley Hoag, I often helped screen prospective summer associates—a traditional test run for entry-level jobs at law firms. Even though it was always an arduous day, interviewing twenty or more candidates, I looked forward to meeting the students and considering each one's potential future. I had made trips like this several times, but in fall 2006, I experienced something new.

Unlike any recruiting trip in the past, I found students with a focus on the larger world outside of law school and law firms. When my peers and I interviewed for our own first jobs out of law school in the 1970s, the conversations were entirely about what we were studying, what we had done in the summer between school years, and what we hoped to accomplish in our legal careers. We talked almost exclusively about the practice of the law. Never in my various interviews with potential employers did I mention that my inspiration to be a lawyer was the character of Atticus Finch in *To Kill a Mockingbird,* a man who simply wants the law to be fairly applied in society. It was that idealism that helped shape my future and encouraged me to explore the highly dramatic politics of the era, including the civil rights, antiwar, and women's movements. These topics, my worldview, and my motivations were rarely, if ever, part of the interview process when I was a young aspiring lawyer.

But at UVA in 2006, I was astonished at the breadth of the students' vision and their willingness to share that with a recruiter. Many had already worked in a wide variety of jobs around the world, some digging wells in the Peace Corps and others analyzing data at the World Bank. One young woman had studied ballet for years, and others had pursued studies in the sciences. They all had arrived at law school with much broader experience in the world than had my generation, and consequently had a more expansive view of career possibilities for themselves—not only in terms of personal success but also in terms of making a positive impact through the practice of law. They wanted to work at a law firm where ethics, integrity, and a sense of social responsibility were clearly enunciated values. And they all, every one, felt passionately about using the law for something bigger than themselves.

> In 2006, I was astonished at the breadth of the students' vision and their willingness to share that with a recruiter.

They were already global citizens, and they changed my impression of what made the "perfect" associate.

Flying back from UVA, I finished reading Thomas Friedman's *The World Is Flat*. Several of the forces Friedman identified as reshaping the world seemed immediately relevant to the students I had just met, namely *connectivity, vast information,* and *collaboration* (all three of which were just converging in the rise of social media). In addition, Friedman observed that all kinds of integrated processes, from manufacturing to transportation, were being separated into distinct, easily copied components. In the new world, everything was globalized . . . and these students understood that idea at a gut level. At a young age, they had traveled extensively, and many had worked abroad.

In the final pages of *The World Is Flat* (second edition), Friedman recalls dropping off his eldest child at college for the first time. He wrote, "I can honestly say it was one of the saddest days of my life. And it wasn't just the dad-and-mom-dropping-their-eldest-child-off-at-school thing. No, something else bothered me. It was the sense that I was dropping my daughter off into a world that was so much more dangerous than the one she had been born into. I felt like I could still promise my daughter her bedroom back, but I couldn't promise her the world—not in the carefree way that I had explored it when I was her age."[1]

I closed the book and realized, *Oh my God, this is what I've just witnessed. I'm seeing those changes in these students and in the young associates at Foley Hoag.* The world Friedman described was profoundly different from the world experienced by my generation, the Baby Boomers, and by those of Generation X, who followed us. We grew up in a world of work that was relatively stable, even predictable. These young people grew up in a world of relentless change.

Friedman didn't just mean that the world was more physically dangerous for his daughters; he had written in his newspaper column that globalization destroyed the vocational "moat" that had surrounded educated Western professionals. Industries like textiles had exited the West for developing nations in the 1980s and 1990s, and by the 2000s, it was the turn of educated professionals to feel new competition. Highly skilled jobs like analyzing medical scans, writing software, and drawing up contracts would be outsourced by US hospitals, tech companies, and law firms to skilled but low-cost professionals in China, India, and other emerging economies.[2] The law students I met were of the same generation as Friedman's daughters, and they too faced a world ready and able to compete for their jobs.

Rather than go into a defensive crouch, however, the members of this generation took an expansive view of their role as global citizens. They saw that open-mindedness and ideals, combined with entrepreneurial spirit, were the way to thrive in the globalized world that they had inherited. This cohort, popularly called the Millennials, had a categorically different view of the world and their place in it.

Back at Foley Hoag, I sometimes sparred with other hiring partners about the candidates' qualifications. I would say, "I don't care if this candidate's GPA isn't as good as the other candidate's! You need to hire this candidate because she has such a holistic view of the world and the practice of law in it. This candidate will lead with her ethics and always do the right thing in her work."

Those students stayed at the top of my mind as I considered another phenomenon taking shape in the early 2000s: the failure of traditional hiring processes to identify the qualities that are most needed at work today. Although I could find individual leaders—attorneys, doctors, executives, and government officials—who understood that we live in a profoundly changed

Although I could find individual leaders—attorneys, doctors, executives, and government officials—who understood that we live in a profoundly changed world, I saw too many institutions stuck in a twentieth-century mind-set while operating in a totally new twenty-first-century reality. world, I saw too many institutions stuck in a twentieth-century mind-set while operating in a totally new twenty-first-century reality. Law firms, hospitals, large corporations, and government agencies—so many of them were still looking for the exact same skills and aptitudes they'd been hiring for years before.

There was one sector I knew that was embracing change, encouraging it, and urgently trying to predict what was coming next. That was the business community, and particularly those companies with a more entrepreneurial focus. With competitive advantage front of mind, far-thinking organizational leaders were alert and ready to take on the flat world.

Books about globalization and creative destruction filled the business best-seller lists. *The Innovator's Dilemma, Moneyball, Blue Ocean Strategy,* and *The Tipping Point* described how industries were coping with tectonic forces by reinventing themselves. At the same time, writers like Daniel H. Pink (*A Whole New Mind*) and Seth Godin (*Tribes*) were diving deep into human behavior and motivation, and finding an eager business audience. That audience was very interested in understanding the next generation, both as potential employees and as potential customers.

The problem at the slower-changing institutions like the legal profession wasn't a fear of new technology; it was that they didn't feel much urgency. The status quo was protected by layers of tradition, incentives, and habits of behavior. Technology certainly brought efficiencies and increased productivity (for example, in legal research), but the professions adopted technologies that conformed to their way of doing things. Email and online calendars might have replaced paper, but habits of learning, serving clients, acquiring revenue, and more remained essentially the same. Lines of authority remained the same as well, and so did openness to new ideas . . . or the lack thereof.

I realized with rising concern that the problem was deeply embedded in the way students prepared for their professions. The education system itself had barely adapted to the new global realities. Those Millennial graduates were different, but the practices of many of the colleges and graduate schools they attended were pretty much the same as those at my undergraduate and law schools, Vassar and UVA, in the 1970s. Colleges and university graduate programs had also added email and web research, but introductory classes were still taught in big rooms, and students still wrote papers or studied business or law cases in brilliant abstractions. There was little hands-on learning during the school year, and almost none in which the stakes might be higher than earning a grade. Only during summer breaks and after graduation were students expected to learn how the world really works, by joining a business, law firm, hospital, or nonprofit. And the technical expertise taught by undergraduate and graduate schools was almost always specialized. The amount of information crammed into a few years of classroom learning meant that classes didn't seem to relate that information to the globalized, interdependent, chaotic, and hyperconnected world that emerged in the 2000s.

Soon I was noticing evidence of this problem everywhere. The best and brightest law students studied little about macroeconomics, finance, or the impact of data analysis. Business students might get one semester of ethics training, but emerge with only a vague notion of how a business career should serve the world (beyond philanthropy). And solutions to problems like gender equality and work-life balance seemed as elusive as ever.

Business education, I thought, could lead the way out of this, if for no other reason than that at various points in history, business had shown itself to be responsive to a rapidly changing world. Over the course of my career, I have served on several corporate boards, worked at the Federal Trade Commission, and served as the economics chief of the Massachusetts state government. I had been exposed to many of the forces business was facing. I had witnessed how businesses change and adapt to survive. In corporate offices and on shop floors, great lessons were being learned, and even passed along through professional education. Business was especially interested in grooming future leaders who might cross traditional lines to solve big-picture problems or create breakthrough products.

Unfortunately, budgets for education and training in the corporate world were on the decline even before the Great Recession, and were then cut dramatically.[3] Many business leaders were reluctant, moreover, to invest in employees who might soon jump to a competitor. As hiring slowed in 2008–2011, managers held out for "supercandidates" who would arrive completely prepared to work, innovate, lead, and deliver profits from day one. Into this environment, business graduates came to corporate or entrepreneurial life with uneven skill sets. For example, technically expert finance majors might possess only rudimentary communication skills—at exactly the time when clear communication across cultures and generations was becoming more important than ever.

Like the business community itself, I had begun to believe that the American system that encouraged de facto "silos" of liberal arts education, business education, and technical education was for the most part underserving its students and the organizational world at large. It delivered technically competent people who were not prepared for the new realities.

The contemporary innovation economy needs both left- and right-brain strengths working together.

Daniel Pink's book *A Whole New Mind* offered key insights into the situation. Discussing the "left-brain" and "right-brain" forms of thinking, he observed that skills and capacities associated with the brain's right hemisphere were particularly important to the new economy. To simplify Pink's conceptual framework: the left brain is specialized for detail, analysis, logic, and data gathering; the right brain is specialized to enable synthesis, storytelling (putting information into context), empathy, creativity, and meaning (assigning significance to information, and seeing the big picture). The contemporary innovation economy needs both left- and right-brain strengths working together.[4]

This was the underlying problem: the silos of business and technical and professional education were still training students to develop those strengths separately, as they had for decades. In undergraduate business and technology programs, and especially in graduate programs in those fields, pressure to confer marketable, quantifiable skills crowded out the broader systems thinking that ultimately makes great innovators and entrepreneurs. There was (and is) so much technical information to master in many fields that there was (and is) never enough time to teach or experience such right-brain skills as creativity and storytelling or to focus on ethical behavior in varying contexts.

Liberal arts majors suffered the opposite problem. The declining number of those majoring in English, history, languages, fine arts, and the like had little exposure to the more left-brain disciplines in the course of their studies. It seemed apparent that exposure to business and technical subjects would broaden their understanding of society, of the world of work, and of the global economy. That broader view would inform their critical thinking in their respective fields. An understanding of international finance, for example, would deepen the historian's view of why nation-states succeed or fail.

Higher education's traditional separation of left-brain and right-brain domains has left graduates ill-prepared for a career landscape characterized by hybrid jobs that mix and match elements of those domains on a daily basis.

The students I met in 2006 were personally ready and eager to face the new realities. They had grown up in the hyperconnected world. They embodied its forces with their global outlook. They challenged the status quo. Their heroes were creative rule-breakers in technology, business, the professions, and the arts. They needed evolved methods of learning that would prepare them with technical skills, work experience, and career management acumen *before* graduation. The more technically minded needed to acquire habits of empathy, big-picture thinking, and the confidence to take risks.

I had worked long enough in the practice of law, in government, in the business world, and in civic development to know that real change happens when people see new opportunities to shake up the status quo. Still, I was not part of the education establishment. My contributions to date for improving how young people prepared for working in the world had come through active participation in K–12 education reform in Massachusetts and working with business associations interested in a more contemporary approach to education policy.

So, when Bentley College (now Bentley University) first tentatively approached me about its open presidency, I was intrigued enough to agree to a conversation. A year earlier, I probably would have laughed and taken a quick pass—I was a *lawyer,* for heaven's sake—but I quickly realized that throughout its history, Bentley had connected to the world in ways different from most colleges. The institution's long-standing approach—the cross-disciplinary integration of liberal arts in the context of teaching business, along with a singular focus on business ethics—captured my imagination. This, I thought, might be the appropriate educational response to a world undergoing such dramatic upheaval. In the ensuing months, I met Bentley trustees, faculty, staff, and students. I grew more excited and convinced that the college was developing one of the models for business education that could truly prepare this generation to take its place in the rapidly changing global economies. I became Bentley's president in July 2007.

> Creating an education system that truly prepares a greater number of young people to compete effectively in a global economy has become a common goal among players in education, business, and public policy throughout the United States.

In the years since then, I have seen tremendous innovation in education by a highly diverse community of thinkers and practitioners in colleges large and small. Professional educators, elected officials, and management superstars have all turned their attention to the evolution of higher education because, like me, they see it as one of the urgent issues of our time. Creating an education system that truly prepares a greater number of young people to compete effectively in a global economy has become a common goal among players in education, business, and public policy throughout the United States.

As a self-confessed policy wonk, I'm adding my contribution to the conversation with this book. I will describe a set of practices that are working at Bentley and other schools. I will share what I've learned from educators and practitioners at the front line of innovation. I will also share what I've learned from students who are putting their futures on the line as they practice a new model we call "hybrid learning," from the Ivy League to community colleges. I will reference hybrid learning throughout this book, and describe it in detail in chapter 6.

There is no single, all-encompassing prescription for curing every ill in higher education today. What works for Vassar and Wesleyan won't be exactly right for UVA, Duke, Baylor, or

Santa Clara College. But a set of principles is emerging that clearly works for many students at many different institutions. These students are graduating well prepared to face the complex world that Friedman chronicled. *The World Is Flat* contained a trenchant description of the most powerful changes sweeping global economies. In the years since the first edition was published in 2005, the phenomena Friedman analyzed, from outsourcing to smartphones, have inspired a national discussion about how American business and education can cope with accelerating change.[5]

His ideas helped motivate my transition into higher education, so I was beyond excited in May 2014 when Friedman was the keynote speaker at the Greater Boston Chamber of Commerce annual meeting. As the former (and first woman) president and member of the executive committee of the Chamber, I was invited to a private reception. And I thought gosh, wouldn't it be cool to meet Tom Friedman! But I also knew there would be a hundred other people there, all movers and shakers in Boston, all vying to chat with the keynote speaker.

But when I arrived that night, I was surprised to see Friedman standing at the back of the room at the bar, chatting alone with my friend Joe Grimaldi, then the chairman of the advertising agency Mullen (now MullenLowe). So I walked back to the bar to say hello to Joe, who then introduced me as the president of Bentley.

Following the introduction, I said, "Mr. Friedman, do you mind if I tell you a personal story?" And I told him the story I recounted earlier of flying back from UVA and reading about his dropping his daughter off at school, and how his book brought together everything that had been stirring at the back of my mind since interviewing those young law students. I told him, "You're responsible for me setting aside my law practice and becoming the president of a business school."

He said something to the effect, "No one's ever told me anything like this before." Maybe no one had told him that, but the tectonic changes he noted in his book (and his subsequent books) have probably changed more lives than he could imagine.

Later that evening, I found that Friedman and I were still on the same wavelength. He started his keynote by saying, "The number one question I get asked these days is, 'How's my kid going to get a job?'"

Bentley is a business university, so this book will focus on business education. Located in the city of Waltham, Massachusetts, nine miles from Boston, Bentley hosts about forty-two hundred undergraduate students and a thousand graduate students in a distinctive fusion of business education and the arts and sciences. Originally an accounting and finance school, Bentley has evolved in recent decades to emphasize the study of liberal arts, technology, ethics, and social responsibility, in addition to the traditional business disciplines. Our track record speaks to the value of a Bentley education, and I'm personally proud that 98 percent of graduates have been either hired or accepted to graduate programs within six months of graduation for the past eight years.[6]

Business administration and management is the number one major in America.[7] In recent years, about 360,000 undergraduates leave school with a business degree—about 19 percent of total bachelor's degrees and twice the number of the runner-up category, health professions. In graduate school, the MBA accounts for 25 percent of master's degrees.[8] With so many students and so many institutions, the teaching of business allows for wide experimentation. At some points, I will advocate for a broader view of undergraduate education overall, talking about how the fusion of liberal arts right-brain thinking and business left-brain thinking works to improve both disciplines. Business education is a terrific place to experiment because it is feeling all the pressures that business feels, acutely and quickly. We in business education hear every day from the company recruiters and executives who want graduates who are genuinely prepared to face today's innovation economy. Business schools are market driven, perhaps more urgently than other disciplines.

Although this book explores new models for undergraduate and graduate business education, it is written in nonacademic language, for a lay readership. I am writing it at a time of wide and necessary national debate about every component of higher education. Talented leaders, journalists, and thinkers are currently applying their thinking to many related issues, including education costs and student debt, the influence for better and worse of college rankings, and the comparative value of "top" versus "middle-tier" universities. I am writing as politicians and policymakers debate wider access to higher education and its influence on contemporary concerns, including income inequality, poverty, and the future of work.

It is tempting to wade deeply into these issues, but they are beyond the scope of this book. Academics, members of the media, and writers as diverse as Fareed Zakaria of CNN, Michael Crow of Arizona State University, Jeffrey Selingo of the *Chronicle of Higher Education*, Michael Roth of Wesleyan University, and Frank Bruni of the *New York Times* are just a sample of serious thinkers who have added their voices to the conversation.

I write this from a different perspective: not as a lifelong academic or journalist but as a passionate player in law, government, business, and policy. I came to academia with respect for its institutions and expertise, in hopes of preserving the best while helping accelerate necessary change. In addition, I hope to contribute meaningfully to the broader conversation around effective models of undergraduate and graduate business education in a rapidly changing world, using Bentley's focus as one reference point.

That perspective informs my work every day at Bentley, and sharing its practical lessons is the reason I wrote this book.

1

HIGHER EDUCATION'S
CHALLENGE TO CHANGE

Dan Merica is a political producer for CNN, a job that brings him into daily contact with the reporters and political players who shape the country's policies. By 2015, he was covering politics and religion from Washington DC, and later he left to cover the presidential candidates in Iowa, New Hampshire, and around the country. The surprising thing about Merica is that he didn't go to college thinking he'd be a journalist. While a student at Bentley University, he took business courses and majored in the arts and sciences–based global studies before going on to earn a master's degree in public affairs at American University. Global studies and public affairs, and then journalism, constitute an unusual career path for a business school graduate, but Dan Merica is a great example of the adaptability of today's students. Like many of his peers, Merica had the passion, energy, and courage to follow an untraditional path from education to career.

Isabel Hirama lived in many countries as a child, because her parents worked in the foreign service. As a teenager, she had summer internships at US embassies. She studied psychology and philosophy at the College of William & Mary, but didn't have any idea what she wanted to do when she graduated in 2014. She ran marketing programs for an international tech start-up and then returned to William & Mary in 2016 to study business analytics. What school experiences gave Hirama the most insight into building the career she has today? She says, "Running the salsa club and changing a service trip from Christian-only to an interfaith learning experience." Her best advice to today's students: "Learn to create something out of nothing."

Brian Schuster went to the University of North Carolina at Chapel Hill. His nontraditional combination of business major and creative writing minor prepared him in unexpected ways for his job today: solutions architect at a technology firm. He says, "When you're in business school, there's a lot of focus on tools and case studies that hope to give you something marketable after college. It's useful, but it misses one of the major points of business—that you're often trying to convince people why your product or service is better than the rest. It's not about your product but how people *perceive* you and your business. In its truest sense, you're telling a story." For all the quantitative analysis he learned, his most valuable business skills for his job today came from a creative writing class. He's a storyteller—with data.

Dan Merica, Isabel Hirama, and Brian Schuster embody the new reality of higher education: The most fruitful experiences of their college and early work years were about crossing boundaries rather than following a traditional path of study and a traditional career beginning. They threw themselves into passionate interests and turned those into marketable skills. And they are today pursuing careers that also transcend traditional job descriptions. Their stories are three examples of "hybrid learning" leading to "hybrid work"—and higher education needs to pay attention. The change from traditional paths of study to hybrid learning is not going to happen in the future: it's already here today.

Higher Education at a Turning Point

If you or someone you care about is thinking about pursuing higher education, you face a national and global outlook dramatically different from that of twenty years ago. College has never been more expensive; the job outlook and "hot jobs" lists change year by year; everything from manufacturing to entertainment to economics is globalized; and only the fabled "1 percent" of families seems secure.

> If you or someone you care about is thinking about pursuing higher education, you face a national and global outlook dramatically different from that of twenty years ago.

Adding to these economic challenges, higher education itself is in the middle of a great transition from its 150-year-old model to something else—and it seems nobody can guarantee precisely what that something else will be ten years from now. Various experts have weighed in on the value of new educational ventures such as online learning and for-profit colleges. Surveys have crunched income data to determine the lifelong monetary value of a degree. Analysts and think tanks have tried to understand the lifelong impact of graduating with huge student loan debts. And policymakers have proposed plans to help students and their families, but then have struggled through the all-too-common political problems of turning ideas into action.

At the confluence of all these big issues lies the simple question, "How *should* a young adult today best prepare for work and life in the coming decades?"

Anyone considering the value of a college education has to ask that question. And even though data prove that higher education remains key to higher earnings,[1] the current generation of students is right to ask, "In addition to higher earning potential, how will college teach me to manage the changes sure to come?"

A further complication facing students and families is that many of today's real-world careers aren't mapped out in advance. Even doctors and lawyers often begin with undergraduate majors in the humanities or arts before pursuing degrees in their field of choice.[2] Dan Merica, Isabel Hirama, and Brian Schuster are just three examples of people whose careers have gone in unexpected directions.

So when we are trying to determine the value of an education, the question quickly turns to *what sort* of preparation is optimal for each individual to take his or her place as an economic and social actor.

Despite the challenges, there is reason for great optimism, both in the new outlook of today's generation of college-age students and in new models of higher education. Higher education institutions are reconsidering how young people can best prepare for career, citizenship, and life in the twenty-first century. Bentley University, where I serve as president, is one school where new practices are in place. It's happening in big, well-known schools like the University of Chicago's Kellogg School of Management and the Haas School of Business at the University of California. It's happening at smaller schools like Olin College, the Alamo Colleges, and Southern New Hampshire University. In one sentence, Gallup's Valerie Calderon sums up what leaders in those and other institutions have learned: "*How* you go to college matters more than *where* you go to college."[3]

Recent surveys by such organizations as Gallup and the Pew Research Center show that students with a certain set of experiences and behaviors thrive when it comes to career and life satisfaction after graduation, and that these experiences and behaviors can be nurtured at a wide range of college types.

How you go to school is the missing question in the debate about the value and return on investment (ROI) of a college education.[4]

> *How* you go to school is the difference between a successful college experience and an unsuccessful one—whether you judge success by income, job satisfaction, or overall happiness.

How you go to school is the difference between a successful college experience and an unsuccessful one—whether you judge success by income, job satisfaction, or overall happiness. It is a critical question for anyone trying to improve the quality of his or her college experience.

How is a critical question for students and parents that should precede the question of *where* to go to college. What kind of learning suits an individual's intellect, temperament, and values?

New York Times columnist Frank Bruni, in his excellent book *Where You Go Is Not Who You'll Be*, points out that the corner offices of Fortune 500 companies are occupied more often by graduates of "second-tier" institutions than name-brand universities.[5]

The undergraduate majors of former big-company CEOs like Boeing's James McNerney (American studies), Bank of America's Brian Thomas Moynihan (history), and Starbucks's

Howard Schultz (communications) show that a liberal arts degree isn't a one-way ticket to underemployment. The same is true in nonbusiness professions like politics and the arts.[6]

Until recently, individual success after college was most often attributed to a student's personal traits, such as perseverance or work ethic. Those are significant, but recent research also establishes that learning methods, habits, and environments help develop both the skills needed in today's workforce and the ability to combine those skills in new ways. By integrating what matters after graduation into the college experience, rather than just measuring GPA or postgraduation income, schools at every level of prestige are learning to do their jobs better.

A recent Bentley University study found that "hybrid jobs"—jobs that combine hard technical skills like computer science with soft "people" skills like empathy and communication—are among the fastest-growing categories of employment today. *Hybrid* describes the mix of skills you'll find in managers at tech companies where engineers and designers mix and combine development responsibilities for a new product. Web managers, for example, need a bit of everything: software coding skills, design skills, and that combination of data orientation and creative empathy that's necessary for understanding "user experience."

The need for people who can thrive in hybrid jobs is growing because the old lines between one kind of work and another are blurring.

The need for people who can thrive in hybrid jobs is growing because the old lines between one kind of work and another are blurring. In the past, a corporate financial manager would be expert in accounting, tax, and other financial disciplines, with perhaps a smattering of legal knowledge. Today she needs to know all that *and* the fundamentals of sustainability, global trade, data analysis, corporate responsibility, and more. Every important financial decision has to consider those issues because they impact financial outcomes.

Today, a marketing manager needs to know how to ask data analysts the right questions. He has to develop the capacity to separate the signal from the noise when examining huge amounts of data. Nurses and nurses' aides, whose great strengths might be in communication and caring, have to operate ever more sophisticated technology.

To prepare for today's workforce, students must practice crossing traditional boundaries *before* they arrive in the workplace. Crossing boundaries takes certain skills and also qualities like adaptability and a willingness to proceed even in an ambiguous situation. These qualities, which I'll detail later, can only be learned by practice. That's one of the key *hows* of higher education today—hybrid jobs require hybrid learning.

How you go to college is also about more than acquiring information. Anyone with a web browser and a minimal investment of time and money can find the raw information taught in most classrooms. Many high-level skills can be learned by the proverbial kid with a laptop in the parents' basement. American business lore is full of self-taught strivers, from Abraham Lincoln reading by the fire to the dropout millionaires of Silicon Valley. But for all the fact that we love that image, these people are rare. In most cases, a college education still happens at college.

How means learning to apply information in real-world situations, with consequences that are higher than a grade. *How* means learning to become engaged in all the issues that might surround a decision. In the old days, you might approach a business situation with the goal of maximizing profit, and that's a fairly straightforward mathematical problem. Now, the emphasis would include the triple bottom line of profit, people (management), and the planet (making the world a better place or at a minimum doing no harm). It's a problem that blurs the old lines separating disciplines.

How also includes life outside the classroom, from residential life to playing sports to teaching kids reading in a local school. These are essential experiences as a student matures and explores her strengths and interests.

The bottom line for how you go to college is this: A successful college career means practicing, over and over, the hands-on work of crossing those boundaries. It demands that you get out of the comfort zone of your natural skills and temperament and embrace the unfamiliar. Because that's exactly what work—and life—is going to demand from you.

> As a practical reality, *where* students go to college strongly influences *how* they go.

As a practical reality, *where* students go to college strongly influences *how* they go. Colleges and universities have unique cultures, just like organizations in business, government, and society. Bentley University is very different from Vassar, where I went to undergraduate school, and both are different from the University of Virginia, where I studied law. Colleges have different worldviews, purposes, and—to use the marketing term—value propositions. Ohio State (OSU) has about fifty-six thousand students—almost ten times as many as Bentley. You can learn the same accounting or writing skills at Bentley and OSU, but the two promise very different college experiences.

What Really Prepares Students for Success

The key factors that make a college education successful these days are coming more and more into focus. Recent reports by the Gallup Organization and Purdue University, supported by the Lumina Foundation, focused closely on these factors. The reports, titled *Great Jobs, Great Lives: The Gallup-Purdue Index Report*, presented results and analysis of information provided by more than thirty thousand college graduates across the United States. (The report is an ongoing project, with results first published in 2014, and I will quote from several editions in this book.) The 2014 Gallup-Purdue report compared schools of all kinds—public and private, small and large, very selective and not very selective. The report's executive summary notes its key finding: "The data presented in this report suggest . . . that [establishing value is found] in thinking about things that are more lasting than selectivity of an institution or any of the traditional measures of college. Instead, the answers may lie in *what* students are doing in college and *how* they are experiencing it. Those elements—more than any others—have a profound relationship to a person's life and career."[7]

Gallup-Purdue found six factors in the undergraduate experience that made a measureable difference in people's well-being after college:[8]

· A professor who made them excited about learning
· Professors who cared about them as a person

· A mentor who encouraged them to pursue their goals
  and dreams

· Work on a project that took a semester or more
  to complete

· An internship that allowed for applying what they were
  learning in the classroom

· Participation in extracurricular activities and organizations in college

How many graduates surveyed said that they had experienced all six of these factors?

Three percent.

Three percent, including students from all kinds of schools,
all kinds of backgrounds and interests, and all over the
United States!

Okay, we've got some work to do.

> The six success factors are best
> achieved in the context of
> place-based education—that is,
> on a campus.

The six success fac-
tors are best achieved in
the context of place-
based education—that
is, on a campus. The
good news is that some
colleges have been
experimenting and re-
fining their educational offerings for years, and many are
focused on improving the experience of college along these
lines. In chapter 4, I'll explore how one-to-one relationships,
hands-on learning, and extracurricular activities such as those
described in the report enable students to cross intellectual

boundaries and grow in both their capabilities and personal vision.

This book intends to add to the conversation by describing a hybrid model of higher education that has proven effective in preparing both business-focused and liberal arts students for life after graduation. Four broad principles shape my case:

1. The innovation economy needs a new graduate.

   This is why business education models must adapt to the changing workplace and macroeconomic realities. For families, understanding the changes that the innovation economy has made to the workplace is the starting point when considering the question, "How is my kid going to get a job?" For educators, understanding the nature of hybrid work confirms the need to combine traditional left-brain and right-brain skills to prepare students for careers after graduation.

2. Students need a new college experience.

   What does it mean to be prepared for career and life? Sources like Bentley's surveys and the Gallup-Purdue Index point to better measures validating a college education, and why how you go to college matters more than where you go to college.

3. A new model must embrace the total college experience.

   The hybrid model breaks traditional barriers between business and liberal arts education, in response to the breaking down of those barriers in the workplace. In particular, I'll show how the components of hybrid learning operate in the four venues of learning (classroom, cohort, community, corporation) in a young person's life before and after graduation.

4. The model must reflect generational change in and out of the workplace.

This means addressing values and challenges of the oft-maligned Millennials and of Generation Z that followed them (see "The Hybrid Generations" in chapter 3), today's students and young adults shaping the world of work, and the education that best prepares them to face it.

Features of Hybrid Learning

Hybrid learning is particularly relevant to the current generation of students. Hybrid is not unique to Bentley; similar curriculum designs are being practiced at the University of Michigan's Stephen M. Ross School of Business, New York University's Stern School of Business, and others. It's inspiring new ways of learning at Olin College, a selective engineering school. Columbia Business School offers its Program on Social Intelligence, and St. Lawrence University's curriculum offerings include a major for business in the liberal arts.[9]

The hybrid model breaks traditional barriers between business and liberal arts education, in response to the breaking down of those barriers in the workplace.

Drawing from educational research, the practices of other colleges and universities, and, most important, the experience of our students, we at Bentley have created a checklist of features that characterize hybrid learning. Throughout this book, I will show how these features operate in higher education. They are not independent of one another; for example, the blend of classroom and hands-on learning noted in item 1 is part and parcel of our model of four-year career education, item 7. Mentoring, item 6, applies to faculty but also to business professionals, item 10. The features do not dictate a single model of hybrid learning, but I believe that, taken together, they form a foundation for the kind of education we need in order to prepare today's students for work and life:

1. Colleges should blend classroom teaching and hands-on learning.

2. Students in all majors should be required to take at least one business course.

3. All students, including business majors, should be required to take liberal arts courses.

4. All students, regardless of major, must learn to apply new information technologies to their fields, now and in the future.

5. Schools should connect cocurricular activities to the course of study, applying both left-brain and right-brain skills outside the classroom.

6. Professors and students should be trained in the practices and responsibilities of mentoring and sponsorship.

7. Career services should begin freshman year and continue through graduation, integrated with a student's course of study.

8. Internships should be mandatory for all students, regardless of major.

9. Business professionals should be connected to the class-room, interacting with students in both lectures and real-world problem solving.

10. Businesses should work closely with colleges to shape the schools' career service offerings and inform the curriculum.

The move to hybrid learning addresses issues that are particular passions of mine:

· The radical changes in employment—hiring, getting a job, and working in business—caused by technology and globalization

· Innovations in curriculum that merge traditionally separate domains of learning (vocational vs. liberal arts, hard vs. soft skills, left-brain vs. right-brain thinking)

· The diversity of teaching and learning models, trending toward a more individualized experience

· The particular needs and interests of Millennials, Generation Z, and women in business education today

The young people who inspired me back in 2006 to become more involved in higher education seem uniquely willing and able to embrace these changes. Their common desire to rede-fine success along a triple bottom line of financial, social, and environmental progress makes them ready as a generation to create permanent change.

Because Bentley is a business university, our model is natu-rally focused on preparing for the world of work, but we are not limited to that alone; we believe with many others that there are four common components of a hybrid education that prepare one for work and life outside of work.

1. The fusion of business and liberal arts study

2. Study paired with real-world experience in the form of internships, corporate immersion classes, study abroad, and/or service-learning

3. A detailed process of career planning and career management skills training, beginning in freshman year

4. Ongoing training in technology skills

These four overall components, working together, form a new experience designed to equip students to thrive in the innovation economy.

My belief in these four components is informed by extensive research, especially the ongoing research done by the Gallup organization and its partners, including *Great Jobs, Great Lives,* and by Bentley's PreparedU project and its surveys, which are ongoing studies dedicated to identifying the most effective methods for preparing students for work and life after graduation.

In these pages, you'll meet people who don't fit the stereotypical image of a business community. You'll meet professor Tim Anderson, an honorary member of the Crow Nation, who uses a traditional talking stick in his sociology class to teach the importance of authenticity. You'll hear from serial entrepreneur Woody Benson as he and his teaching partner Perry Lowe turn a class into a real-life consulting firm for a start-up.

You'll meet current students like Usama Salim, who is studying business and liberal arts while preparing for a medical career, and graduates like Will Markow, who started out as a professional boxer but ended up studying quantitative analysis.

You will also meet professional educators from across the country who are leading a revolution in how we prepare students for career and life. People like Dr. Paul J. LeBlanc, president of Southern New Hampshire University and champion of competency-based education, a new model for lifelong learning. People like Dr. Bruce Leslie, who is changing the culture of five colleges in Texas through a deep intellectual partnership with Franklin Covey Company's 7 Habits of Highly Effective People program. And people like John Colborn of the Aspen Institute, who is rethinking the ways that employers, students, and colleges can work together to make business education deliver what business needs.

All of them embody a new way of making the most out of higher education, with a new vision of *how* to prepare for the postgraduation reality of constant change, merging disciplines, and the blurring lines between work and life.

2

YESTERDAY'S EDUCATION MEETS TODAY'S WORLD

Katherine Dayton never thought she'd run a business. When she left her native Montana for Dickinson College in Pennsylvania, her main interests were basketball and environmental science. "Environmental science was just a certificate program at the time," she remembers, "so I had to pick a major to go along with it, and I chose policy studies. I was kind of a black sheep with a group that was headed for government after graduation. On top of that, I was the only Montanan in my graduating class!"

Nevertheless, Dayton was named policy studies student of the year. Even though she wasn't headed for Washington DC like many of her classmates, her passion for two widely different areas of study gave her the confidence to experiment with career paths. "I wanted to work creatively," she says. "I learned that my career would take some bends and diversions along the way."

At Dickinson, religion professor Mara Donaldson jolted Dayton's idea of what she would do later in life. "You want a job," said Professor Donaldson, "but I want you to change the world!" Nobody had said that to her before. The words stuck as Dayton tried several career fields, and then she went to work for VISIONS, a company that managed service trips abroad for high school youth. The Montanan found her mission—to challenge young people with hard-working service trips in poor areas.

Dayton still didn't think of herself as a businesswoman, but she returned to Montana, earned an MBA, and then bought VISIONS, which she owns and runs today.

⸺

> If the college environment encourages students to adopt a view of life after graduation that is less like a plan and more like a narrative, they will be open to acting on unexpected opportunities.

Katherine's story is one of many I know which show that the most influential moments in college can arrive unplanned. How a student responds to those moments can make the difference between following a conventional career path and finding the courage to step on the road less taken. If the college environment encourages students to adopt a view of life after graduation that is less like a plan and more like a narrative, they will be open to acting on unexpected opportunities.

My story is more traditional than Dayton's, but it has had its share of surprises. I might say that my career path unfolded in spite of the well-plotted plans typical of my generation.

I graduated from Vassar College in 1972. Our commencement speaker was Hanna Holborn Gray, a historian who would soon become the first female president of a major American university (the University of Chicago—*after* fourteen months as the interim president of Yale). My classmates, like every graduating class I've ever seen, were young and energetic and idealistic.

After two years working in human resources, I applied to law school, telling my parents that even four years of the best undergraduate education I could have imagined left me with no truly concrete skill sets. That's how we thought of the liberal arts in 1972. We were wrong. In fact, Vassar had taught me how to think critically, conduct research, and communicate.

But I confess that my friends and I spent very little time as undergraduates thinking about how we would fit into the professional world, how to pursue our passions and build a career, and ultimately how to make a difference in the world. Nobody talked about "lifelong learning" or acquiring new skills on a continuous basis. Vassar did have a skeletal career office, but I don't recall ever consulting the staff there. I did recently come across a form from the college's career services staff asking what I had done the summer before (probably for information purposes).

Many of us attended graduate school because we thought of it as the place to learn a "real" profession. Those who wanted to teach at universities went on to get doctorates. More, like me, went to professional schools to pursue law, business, medicine, government, and the like. (That cohort even included artists: Meryl Streep, Vassar '71, continued her education at the graduate Yale School of Drama. Her classmate, Pulitzer Prize–winning novelist Jane Smiley, went on to earn an MFA and PhD at the University of Iowa's famous writing program.)

Colleges encouraged us to take this view. For generations, elite undergraduate institutions saw themselves as cathedrals of pure learning. Many majors existed in their own intellectual worlds.

Students and faculty engaged the great social questions of the day—civil rights, the Vietnam War, the women's movement, the War on Poverty, and more—but these activities were reactions to the times, not part of a formal education. Vassar's great institutional questions at the time were whether to evolve from a women's college to a coeducational institution on its own (it did), and whether to move its physical location from Poughkeepsie, New York, to merge with Yale University in New Haven, Connecticut (it didn't).

Even though most Americans agreed that education was important, there wasn't much hard data on the value of an education. If colleges like Vassar or Yale kept records of how their graduates progressed in career or life achievements, it was for the purposes of affinity and alumni fundraising, not for determining whether students' investment of time or money had been worthwhile. No one referred to college in terms of its return on investment. Its value was simply accepted.

In the past few decades, the pace of change in business, science, medicine, and other disciplines has accelerated. Driven by the forces of creative destruction, globalization, and technology, many sectors of the economy have adapted at an incredible pace. This has been especially true of business, where the Darwinian motto has long been "evolve or die."

During this same period, higher education has tended to change more slowly. It adopted computers and advanced laboratories and new subjects to study, but the experience of college—classroom lectures followed by homework—has stayed pretty stable. At Vassar, we had many seminars and smaller classroom courses with a discussion approach to learning as well as longer term papers as the homework. This has long been typical of smaller undergraduate schools beyond the first-year survey courses.

The Historical Missions of Higher Education

For generations, Americans accepted three grand and distinct missions for higher education: vocational preparation, academic leadership, and—for want of a more precise term—producing well-rounded citizens and promoting leadership across society.

Vocational preparation in the broadest sense is focused on the student as an economic player. This idea that organizations would prepare individuals with applied knowledge and skills is as old as the craft guilds of the Middle Ages. At the top of the American educational-vocational system, undergraduate study led to a career or to graduate school, from which students emerged ready to take their place in law or medicine or business.

College 150 years ago was a place where the rich and powerful sent their sons and (sometimes) daughters to take their place at the top of society. After World War II, the G.I. Bill made college the place America sent its returning soldiers. They reentered the workforce with more education and joined the world's mightiest economy. In the last thirty years, as globalization has sent unskilled or semiskilled jobs overseas, many Americans looked to college as the key to understanding and learning the skills and technical knowledge needed for an economy that required more of both for a person to land a decent job.

> For the majority of students and their parents, the career advantage of holding a degree is still the most compelling reason to attend college.

For the majority of students and their parents, the career advantage of holding a degree is still the most compelling reason to attend college, and answers the question of whether their investment of time and money will be paid off in job satisfaction and higher lifelong earnings. The facts back this up. In 2014, the Federal Reserve Bank of San Francisco published a report estimating that by retirement, "the college graduate would have made about $830,800 more than the high school graduate."[1]

Today's college degree has become the equivalent of yesteryear's high school diploma—a minimum educational requirement to land a good job. Jobs once labeled "low skill" are becoming more complex and require new skills (especially technical skills), and many employers now require a bachelor's degree for positions that in the past were filled by non-degree-holding candidates.[2] Robotics and other technologies have changed or eliminated lower-skill jobs like assembly line work.

Beyond vocational training, a broad consensus in the twentieth century held that the nation was well served by a college system that advanced knowledge through research.

Academic leadership is the mission that, in popular culture, confers great prestige on a university. Research universities, especially, advance pure and applied knowledge in many disciplines, whether engineering or financial analysis or anthropology. Research universities regularly announce new discoveries, inventions, and insights. The Internet, artificial intelligence, economic models, medical breakthroughs, nano-technology, the human genome map, and other accomplishments too numerous to list began as university research projects.

Academic leadership in the form of research and discovery shaped the careers of generations of professors (the old truism of "publish or perish" as a path to tenure). At many universities, it exists in awkward opposition to the teaching mission for the simple reason that research is about acquiring new knowledge, whereas teaching means repeating current knowledge. The respected researcher has less time to teach, goes the argument, and shouldn't be required to spend time teaching undergraduates the basics. Great faculty manage this dilemma through personal dedication and talent, but it is nevertheless a structural hazard of the profession.

The third traditional mission of college is *producing well-rounded and able citizens.* College is an academy of citizenship and intellectual development, qualities embodied in the liberal arts courses of study—language, literature, history, social sciences, and the arts. Education in the liberal arts prepares women and men to be engaged citizens, with the cultural knowledge and hard-to-quantify skills that contribute to an ethical, socially conscious civilization as well as to an economy.

Dr. Jonathan M. White, director of the Bentley Service-Learning and Civic Engagement Center and associate professor of sociology, states the case clearly: "Higher education exists not only to shape the employees of our future but to shape the torch holders of our society's future. And if anybody thinks that's controversial, that this is not what education is supposed to be about, then they don't understand what higher education was invented for, or how *incredibly* important it is."

All three missions serve a useful national (and global) purpose. All three have a noble and vital role in the lives of students and the advancement of civilization—economically, politically, technologically, and morally. And what interests me are the ways that new models of higher education can advance all three missions in today's hyperconnected, globalized, ultra-competitive world, and in particular how business education can do this.

The Rise of ROI Education

For-profit businesses have more dynamic life cycles than colleges. Of the companies producing extraordinary long-term value that business guru Jim Collins identified in 2001 in his book *Good to Great*, several have become bankrupt, been swallowed up, or changed beyond recognition.[3] In his 2009 book *How the Mighty Fall*, Collins said that eleven of the sixty *Good to Great* companies fell to "mediocre or worse" in the decade after his initial study.[4]

Universities and colleges are less susceptible to the Darwinian forces of business, but they are not immune to those forces. They compete for customers (students), generate revenue, hire employees, and balance budgets. But until recently, they seemed immune to the laws of survival. When a business with five thousand employees goes bankrupt, it's national news for a day or two. When a university closes, as Antioch College in Ohio did from 2008 to 2011,[5] the event sparks existential debate in the media and on campuses alike.

College costs have risen steeply in recent decades, and the amount of student debt outstanding in the United States is worrisome. The troubles that Millennial graduates had finding first jobs after the last recession tested people's faith in the economic value of a degree. Anyone involved in running a college today—faculty, staff, executive, or trustee—knows the cross-currents and debates: academic flexibility versus teaching a core curriculum; paying for first-rate faculty and facilities versus containing costs; encouraging broad inquiry versus teaching specific job skills.

> Driven by the rising cost of education and other economic realities, students and families have by necessity taken a consumerist attitude toward college.

Driven by the rising cost of education and other economic realities, students and families have by necessity taken a consumerist attitude toward college. They no longer ask only, "Should I attend college?" but now also ask, "What's the return on my investment of time, talent, and money in this particular institution?" Those fortunate enough to afford tuition outright often have the luxury of weighing one college against another in terms of personal fit, potential achievement, or proximity to home. Those who borrow large sums of money to attend college are more likely to make a choice based on assumed debt against increased earning potential and life satisfaction.

The strategy for choosing the right college now resembles choosing a personal investment strategy. The financial stakes are so high, it's no wonder a large "advice industry" has grown up around college admissions counseling.

Chuck Hughes, founder and president of the college counseling service Road to College, notes that those statistics about lifetime income play into a consumerist narrative that can cause a great deal of anxiety among students and parents. That pressure is manifest at different income levels. Says Hughes,

> It's difficult to sit with some families whose parents have financial resources to pay for the full cost of a university, which can exceed $60,000 per year. Many want the name-brand college with the highest ranking. They want prestige. They want the BMW, Gucci bags, and other designer labels. They want their name-brand college too, and it's difficult to persuade them that maybe, maybe it doesn't matter so much where their children go to college but more what they make of their college degree and experience.
>
> Then there are the families who may or may not qualify for financial aid . . . suburban or urban families whose children attend affluent high schools or private schools. They believe a name-brand school will better position their kid in the future, even though studies show time and again most Fortune 500 executives didn't have to attend a prestige school.
>
> And then you've got the families who are the core of America, with incomes around $50,000 to $75,000, and they absolutely can't afford private college without significant financial aid. They ask, "Do I save for my retirement and limit my children's debt, or stretch to afford a private college on the assumption that they'll get a *better* education?"

Hughes and his counselors start with the facts about each college in question. They cite postgraduation job placement rates and the availability of debt-free financial aid, but Hughes admits that he's fighting the general impression that attending a name-brand college automatically means having a better life.

College rankings from media outlets like *U.S. News, Money,* the *Wall Street Journal* and countless others that seem to pop up out of the woodwork every year add to students' and parents' anxiety with an implicit message of objective superiority. The rankings have their uses, especially if you understand their different methodologies, but what consumer can easily understand why Duke University ranks number 7 in one survey and number 26 in another?[6] What difference would that make for an individual student's experience at that college? And which criteria are most relevant to the individual? In 2015, the Brookings Institution created a "value-added" ranking of colleges that placed lesser-known colleges such as Rose-Hulman Institute of Technology in Indiana and SUNY Maritime College in New York in their top ten.[7] The Brookings model is a provocative response to college-ranking obsession, and adds the larger point that how you rank depends on what you measure.

Preparing for Work in the Twenty-First Century

John Seely Brown was the chief scientist of Xerox Corporation and director of its legendary Palo Alto Research Center (PARC). He's also known as one of America's most innovative organizational thinkers. In a video for the knowledge forum Big Think, he described his far-reaching view of preparing for a career, saying, "I would rather hire a high-level World of Warcraft player than an MBA from Harvard."[8]

Brown was talking about how people work, learn, and lead in what he terms the "Exponential Age"—a time of change so rapid that it cannot be managed by traditional means. He noted that devotees of the massive multiplayer online game World of Warcraft have personal passion, democratic and meritocratic social systems, curiosity, and openness to criticism and ideas. Their skills cross traditional boundaries: they tend to be both technically adept *and* imaginative, narrative driven *and* data driven. They are prepared by temperament and talent to participate in an endlessly changing environment.

Does that description of a sought-after employee sound familiar? Welcome to the world of business in the twenty-first century. To chart a practical course forward for business education, we need to put it in the context of changing social and economic conditions. One of the most insightful reporters of those changes is columnist Thomas Friedman.

As I mentioned in the introduction to this book, I met Friedman when he spoke at the Greater Boston Chamber of Commerce annual meeting in 2014. He described a convergence of forces so consequential that educational and business leaders are barely beginning to wrap their minds around its meaning.

Friedman said that the most important thing to happen in the early twenty-first century was the merger of globalization and the information technology revolution. He called the move from connected to hyperconnected a "Gutenberg-scale moment"—that is, a giant inflection point that is changing businesses, schools, communities, and institutions everywhere, all at once.

> *How is my kid going to get a job during this Gutenberg-scale moment?* is the question that keeps parents up at night.

How is my kid going to get a job during this Gutenberg-scale moment? is the question that keeps parents up at night. It is the question that any educator should ask when she is tempted to accept the educational status quo, because Friedman is right—every business and every school is changing or will be changed by the forces of globalization and the information technology revolution.

Massive, Open, and Online

Many articles and books in the past few years have explored the possibility that online learning platforms like free MOOCs (massive open online courses) will eventually supplant the place-based university for a significant portion of students. The real-world performance of MOOCs at this point is mixed. Many courses are popular, especially overseas. High-quality online courses are expensive to create, and after offering an initial burst of free courses, many of the top university and MOOC organizations now charge fees for taking a course or receiving a "certificate of completion." At this point, however, there is no consensus in the business community as to whether completing a set of online courses produces competencies equivalent to attending college (which is why competency-based education is gaining in popularity, as we will see in chapter 6).[9]

Rob Lippincott witnessed many of the recent changes as senior vice president for education at PBS, and before that at Pearson and Discovery Education. He was teaching educational technology at Harvard in the early 1980s, and in his business career worked at one of America's earliest Internet companies. His experience makes him a shrewd observer of the unpredictable changes that technology brings to education, most recently in the form of MOOCs. Lippincott notes that in the early days of MOOCs, around 2008–2010, enthusiasts predicted they would render college obsolete. Now those predictions have given way to a more complex scenario.

"In the long run, what MOOCs really mean, *massive* and *open,* is really interesting," says Lippincott. "'Massive' means reaching unprecedented numbers of people. 'Open' might be the real root of innovation, because it's the basis of learning [similar to] a business. You'll see online learning in the moment it's needed, easily digested over a couple of hours. You will join professional learning communities."

Lippincott believes that MOOCs will diversify and merge with other learning experiences, in the way that consumer products continuously change: "What is currently known as a MOOC is a kind of experiment. It's like the first wheel: it rolls. But soon you'll have radial tires and all-weather tires and racing bikes and mountain bikes—sizes, shapes, adaptations. Then we'll see changes in pedagogy . . . how courses are thought of and how they're experienced."

The evolution of MOOCs is under way, as universities, investors, and students explore new platforms and models. Coursera, one of the largest MOOC providers, has received tens of millions in funding as it grows internationally.[10] EdX (www.edx.org), which was founded by Harvard and MIT in

2012, now offers more than a thousand courses online, drawing from ninety universities and other institutions. Recently, the University of Pennsylvania and a company called Steppingstone Scholars even offered a free course for high school students called "How to Apply to College"![11]

The New Keys to Success

The Gallup-Purdue Index was begun as a response to the public desire that higher education institutions become more accountable in how they prepare graduates for a good job and a better life. Building on the intellectual framework of the "Gallup 12" measures of engagement in the workplace and on the Gallup-Healthways Well-Being Index, Gallup surveyed graduates of various schools from the perspective of whether their education led them to an engaging job *and* a holistic sense of well-being (based on five dimensions of well-being: career/purpose, social, financial, community, and physical). Gallup's work is so relevant that I share three of the key findings here:[12]

· *Work engagement is a powerful indicator of career success.*
  It means that a person is emotionally attached and committed to work. It also means better work performance.
  According to the 2014 Gallup-Purdue Index report,
  mentioned in chapter 1, "If an employed graduate had a
  professor who cared about them as a person, one who
  made them excited about learning, *and* had a mentor who
  encouraged them to pursue their dreams, the graduate's
  odds of being engaged at work more than doubled. *Only
  14% of graduates have had all three.*" (Italics mine.)

· *Experiences both inside and outside the classroom are linked to long-term well-being.* In terms of well-being, "Higher well-being is related to graduates' experiences. Graduates who felt 'supported' during college (that professors cared, professors made them excited about learning, and had a mentor) are nearly three times as likely to be thriving than those who didn't feel supported."

· *Most college graduates aren't giving their institutions a passing grade for preparedness.* Overall, only 29 percent of college graduates "strongly agree" that college prepared them well for life outside of college.

The report identified specific college experiences that contributed to enhanced workplace engagement:

· If employed graduates feel that their college prepared them well for life outside of it, the odds that they are engaged at work rise nearly three times. Experiences in college that particularly contribute to feeling prepared for life after college include internships or jobs where students are able to apply what they are learning in the classroom, active involvement in extracurricular activities and organizations, and working on a project that took a semester or more to complete.

· Employed graduates are more likely to be engaged in the workplace if they had any of the three aforementioned experiences, and if they took part in all three, their odds of engagement more than doubled. Among graduates who experienced all three, 59 percent are engaged at work, compared with 30 percent of those who did not have any of these experiences.

· Only 6 percent of all college graduates strongly agree that they experienced all three. Roughly one-third strongly agreed that they worked on a long-term project (32%), and fewer than three in ten strongly agreed that they had an internship or job (29%) or were actively involved in extracurricular activities (20%).

Changing for Good

The changes that are now taking place in higher education are happening because educators are listening to their customers more than ever before. The forces outside the university are coming together to demand that college do a better job of preparing students for what comes after graduation. The cost of college and the competition for the best jobs have given new urgency to this demand, and there's also a cultural element that today's students have brought to the discussion. They are willing to question traditional ways of learning, more so than any generation before them. They are more adaptable to changes in learning techniques and technologies. They are acutely aware of the consequences of debt—many of them because their families suffered the consequences of overborrowing after the 2008–2009 financial crisis.

The revolution in learning will be driven not by fear but by hope of a better way to fulfill the original mission of college.

The change won't be uniform or immediate. Elite and name-brand schools will still attract a large number of applicants. Their endowments, alumni base, and other advantages can shield them from some of the market's demands, at least for a while. But the best of them are already changing: University leaders are not living in an ivory tower but urgently modernizing their curriculums and technologies. Look no further than edX, the joint project of some of the world's finest universities to put free courses online. The revolution in learning will be driven not by fear but by hope of a better way to fulfill the original mission of college.

Community colleges, always focused on vocational outcomes, have been particularly receptive to bringing education and business together. Dr. Bruce Leslie, chancellor of the Alamo Community Colleges in San Antonio, Texas, is integrating the popular business framework of the Franklin Covey Company. He says, "We're using the 7 Habits of Highly Effective People as our primary vehicle both for our students *and* for our employees. We have adopted Principle-Centered Leadership because we believe those skills will make students more successful in college and after."

Leslie recalls an unprompted affirmation that his approach is working:

> I was at a car wash a couple months ago. I went in to pay my bill, and there was a young man standing in front of me talking to the clerk. And he was telling her, 'I'm a student at the Alamo Colleges, and I'm involved in the Student Leadership Institute, and we're studying the 7 Habits, where we learn to be proactive in our work and lives. We learn about synergy and all that stuff.'"
>
> I'm a fly on the wall; he doesn't know who I am. And yet he spontaneously is telling this young lady at the desk that he's doing all this. I paid my bill and introduced myself

to him. "Tell me about this thing!" I said. "Why are you so excited about the 7 Habits?" He said, "Look, I'm an African American kid from Oklahoma. I have no family here; I have nobody here in Texas. And if I didn't have the skill sets that I've gained from the 7 Habits, there's no way I could be successful here. I would have flunked out this past year; I would have had to go home. Instead, it's given me the tools and discipline to be responsible for myself, to take ownership of all the things that I need to do." I couldn't have had a better affirmation that this approach changes lives.

Leslie and others working in community colleges strike me as especially open to innovation because they are more exposed to change than are large private institutions. He lists four factors driving the latest changes: declining financial support for higher education since the Great Recession; the impact of technology; greater activism on the part of students compared to recent decades; and the life situations of community college students, who are more likely than other students to have job and family responsibilities in addition to schoolwork. He says, "Community college students have so many life issues because they're predominantly adults, they're predominantly challenged by family and work and whatever issues they've got, and, of course, we're dealing with a lot of veterans."

Some of the most exciting rethinking of business education is taking place today in graduate schools, undoubtedly because they are more market sensitive than undergraduate colleges. The best thinkers in management education are keenly aware of changes sweeping the workplace—changes in *what* is most important to success and *how* work is being accomplished. Liberal arts disciplines like psychology are playing a greater part in MBA programs than ever before—for example, when studying the importance of emotional intelligence in management decisions. MBA programs that used to stick to written case studies about past situations are instead partnering with companies to bring immediate, tangible problems into the classroom, combining classroom theory and field practice.

And the current generation of students is suited by background and temperament to make the most of these kind of changes. I'll discuss this group—Millennials and Generation Z—in detail in chapter 7.

The debate about whether higher education should be focused more on creating a well-rounded, broadly informed citizen or on preparing for a specific vocation is neither settled nor particularly relevant to this book. It is an "or" question, and I am interested in "and" answers. Auditors should understand market dynamics *and* persuasive communication. Graphic designers are more effective when they understand color theory *and* customer segmentation. Specialization is appropriate as jobs require deeper expertise, but at work, excellence typically combines special knowledge *and* broad understanding.

Liberal arts colleges like Vassar should, for example, encourage every single student to study history *and* become familiar with the basic principles of macroeconomics, whatever his or her major. I tell every student and parent I meet: college is a time to find your passion and pursue your dreams, but you'd better know how to read a balance sheet when trying to determine whether your dream company can take off. Paired with internships, robust career planning, and state-of-the-art technology, hybrid learning will provide students with a good foundation for their long path through career, citizenship, and life.

3

THE INNOVATION ECONOMY NEEDS A NEW GRADUATE

China Gorman, former CEO of the Great Place to Work Institute, has for years been a close observer of the connections between *preparing* for work and *being* at work. She describes the danger of the old paradigm of separating the left-brain/right-brain learning domains:

> We need to end up in a place where you are able to access the strengths you have on each side of your brain as it is appropriate. You have to integrate and pull the best from what you've got, without falling on constructs that say you have to pick one set of strengths. I think we're frequently presented with false choices, and when society or government [or business] says it's one or the other I say, "Wait, wait, wait—why can't we start from the premise that I understand your strengths, and you understand mine, and together we make it better—in education, business, politics, and society?"

When I talk to business leaders around the country, they typically mention a disconnect between how colleges educate undergraduates for business, and the reality of how business operates today. This is the beginning of a healthy dialogue that is encouraging colleges to prepare students for boundary-crossing jobs. David Lucey, vice president of talent acquisition at global marketing company Epsilon, says, "As a corporate

> When I talk to business leaders around the country, they typically mention a disconnect between how colleges educate undergraduates for business, and the reality of how business operates today. This is the beginning of a healthy dialogue that is encouraging colleges to prepare students for boundary-crossing jobs.

recruiter, I have noticed that more colleges and universities are listening to our feedback and are equipping students with the hard and soft skills needed to succeed in the workplace. As a result, graduates are coming into the work environment with a lot more confidence than we have seen in years past."[1] Lucey adds, "While we have made a lot of headway in preparing students, there is no doubt that there is still work to be done. I still believe today's graduates need even more exposure to real work experience."

Since around 2000, business leaders have challenged business educators to enhance the content of their curriculum. Now they want graduates with much more than technical skills. Yes, business graduates still have to understand finance, marketing, and various technologies, but they also need to develop more deeply the skills traditionally associated with the liberal arts—communication, empathy, creativity, esthetics, and psychological insight—because those skills are equally important for most business leaders. Businesses need people who have studied languages, not only to communicate overseas but because language study opens graduates' experience to non-US cultures.[2]

Bentley University's research in *The PreparedU Project: An In-depth Look at Millennial Preparedness for Today's Workforce* confirms recent improvement. In the first survey, more than half of business decision makers and corporate recruiters gave colleges and universities a grade of C or lower on preparing recent college grads for their first jobs.[3] Tellingly, 41 percent of college students themselves agreed with that grade. Three years later, 78 percent of employers believed that recent graduates were "prepared for pursuing a career after college."[4]

What changed? Bentley's survey found that educators listened to business: They saw the shifts in the job market and the growing need for students to develop both hard and soft skills. They recognized the importance of real-world work or field experience in combination with classroom experience and adjusted their curriculums accordingly. They put more emphasis on group projects and teamwork, and focused more strongly on new and emerging technologies. In one example of the forces driving change, 87 percent of educators surveyed said that job market trends were influencing curriculum changes. And 91 percent responded that new technologies influenced curriculum changes and/or course offerings.[5]

A major reason for the influence of both job market changes and new technologies on education was neatly summarized by education reformers Tony Wagner and Ted Dintersmith in 2015 in their book *Most Likely to Succeed*. They wrote, "The world simply no longer cares how much you know, because Google knows everything. What the world cares about—what matters for learning, work, and citizenship—is what you can *do* with what you know."[6]

There's more still to be done. Employers tell us that today's recent graduates have the opportunities and education that rival previous generations. But as Wagner and Dintersmith claim, preparation is no longer solely a matter of what students learn in the classroom. What's gaining currency is the notion of an extended classroom that includes real-world experience that truly prepares graduates to succeed. In their courses, students should find opportunities to interact with corporate partners, learn technologies that will give them an edge in specific industries, and work on group projects that hone collaboration and communications skills. All of these experiences prepare students to succeed in the working world.

How can a business college best prepare its students for a career, given all the changes that have taken place in the past two decades? How can we make the connections between technical skills like writing computer code or managing a financial portfolio, and the broader, nontechnical requirements of business—the skills that produce leadership, adaptability, and innovation?

I'm a public policy wonk. Even when I was practicing law, I spent my time focused on education, environmental, and other broad-based societal issues. One of the best qualities of policy work is that it forces you to take the long view. Policy requires you to assemble a constituency; work with government, civic, and business leaders; and keep your eye on the goal, often for years. Sometimes the pace of change is painstakingly slow, but public policy ultimately has tremendous impact on people's lives.

Work in higher education is similar, and the impact of university research and education on students, society, and the economy is impossible to overstate. Our choices about how to educate students will influence business and the world of work for years to come. If we create educational models and policies that both answer the needs of business now and anticipate long-term trends, we are doing our job well.

And we need to change to do our job well, because today's economy needs a new kind of graduate.

More than ever before, business needs employees with open minds, broad understanding, and respect for knowledge outside their specialized areas of expertise. The great management thinker Peter Drucker wrote that "far too many people—especially people with great expertise in one area—are contemptuous of knowledge in other areas or believe that being bright is a substitute for knowledge."[7] His warning against such thinking should be memorized by today's business student. Although excellent performance often demands deep expertise in one area, business jobs today are characterized by an interdependence of disciplines, skills, outlooks, and even temperaments.

Graduates who embrace this interdependence acknowledge the convergence of big, complicated forces in business. Those forces include the speed of change, the increasing relative importance of innovation, the presence of four generations in the workplace, and a host of new job requirements.

The need to cross traditional intellectual boundaries in preparation for life after college was a key finding of the PreparedU project. The survey found, for example, that business decision makers and corporate recruiters regard so-called soft skills and attitudes as more important for long-term success than the hard skills typically associated with business education.[8]

The term *hard skills* is commonly associated with technical knowledge, logic, quantification, abstraction, and analysis—what Daniel Pink noted as "left-brain" qualities. Conversely, *soft skills* are associated with emotional intelligence, imagination, qualification, and synthesis—the domain of "right-brain" thinking.

To assign value to the domains—that hard skills are more important in managing the necessary tasks of business and that soft skills should be reserved for "relationship" work—leads us into a maze of unhelpful biases. Dr. Bruce Leslie of the Alamo Colleges makes a useful distinction when he says, "In the marketplace, the term *soft skills* has been used traditionally to speak to those skills that students need to have when they leave college in order to be effective in an organization, to be able to be an entrepreneur, to be able to help a company they would go to work for to be competitive."

I like the term *professional skills* to distinguish the skills and knowledge most important to business, whether hard or soft skills. The common distinctions between hard and soft skills are nevertheless convenient when discussing why business and education need to concern themselves with both domains.

What Makes an Effective Employee?

Bentley's PreparedU research found broad agreement among leaders about what qualities are important for success: 84 percent of business leaders (including corporate recruiters) chose integrity. Other highly prized qualities identified by the survey included professionalism (75 percent), positive attitude (75 percent), oral communication skills (71 percent), and working well as a team player (71 percent). Survey respondents put industry and job-specific skills at the bottom of the list, with only 40 percent saying that such technical knowledge skills are important to success in the workplace.

A recent study by the Association of American Colleges and Universities (AACU) detailed similar beliefs. That study's list of the most important attributes in recent graduates are written and oral communication, teamwork skills, ethical decision making, critical thinking, and the ability to apply knowledge in real-world settings.[9]

A quick glance at these data would seem to confirm that soft skills are the real key to success, but dig deeper and you find that business is highly conflicted on that point. When it comes to hiring, 65 percent of business leaders and corporate recruiters say they would prefer to hire recent graduates with industry-specific skills who might be slower to advance, rather than take on liberal arts graduates who need to be trained in industry-specific skills. In other words, business leaders say they value soft skills the most, but base hiring decisions on hard skills.

Why the contradiction? Are business executives just trying to have it all and holding out for "supercandidates" for every position, as they were inclined to do following the Great Recession? Or is something in the hiring system causing them to act against their stated preference?

One reason for the contradiction is a widespread, misleading concept of what makes an effective employee. Industry-specific skills like knowing how to write computer code or apply tax regulations are easy to confirm by testing, so managers default to seeking those skills. It's harder to measure someone's ability to create an innovative solution to a problem, stick diligently and flexibly with his idea, and persevere until the problem is solved.

We also tend to think of integrity, professionalism, positive attitude, and teamwork as character traits. But that's only partially true. Studies in organizational psychology confirm that these traits are also the result of conscious choices and are often influenced by workplace culture. They can be taught and learned, and they should be part of undergraduate preparation for postgraduate life.

Laszlo Bock, who for more than ten years led Google's people function (what most companies call human resources), started in 2007 to identify qualities that makes a person successful at Google. As you'd expect, general cognitive ability and leadership top the list. After that, according to Bock, they found attributes like enjoying fun, intellectual humility (which helps learning), conscientiousness, comfort with ambiguity, and evidence that someone had taken courageous or interesting paths in life.

At the bottom of the list of success factors was role-related knowledge—for example, technical skills. In his 2015 book *Work Rules!* Bock wrote, "Our experience is that curious people who are open to learning will figure out the right answers in almost all cases, and have a much greater chance of creating a truly novel solution."[10]

Bock's analysis, and his long record of hiring success at one of the world's most creative companies, points to a new reality of the innovation economy: the need for higher education to break down traditional barriers between hard and soft skills.

> Liberal arts study emphasizes critical thinking, complex problem solving, empathy, creativity, and communication skills. These are necessary in today's interdependent work environment.

Liberal arts study emphasizes critical thinking, complex problem solving, empathy, creativity, and communication skills. These are necessary in today's interdependent work environment. Defenders of liberal arts education point out that, like the qualities for success, these abilities are enduring needs in business. In the long run, they help make an employee productive throughout a career, no matter how technologies or business models change. In the words of *New York Times* columnist Frank Bruni, "it's impossible to put a dollar value on a nimble, adaptable intellect, which isn't the fruit of any specific course of study and may be the best tool for an economy and a job market that change unpredictably."[11]

Examples of the need for these skills are everywhere, not only in the obvious places like high-tech manufacturing but also in traditional businesses. For example, paralegals must have keen talents for research, writing, and organization, and also must interact with clients in emotionally stressful discussions. Nurses in a modern hospital ward must monitor complex diagnostic information arriving wirelessly from patient rooms, and then leave the screens behind to comfort a distraught patient or family member. Businesses of all kinds need managers who critically synthesize data, priorities, team skills, and company values and apply them in creative ways to projects or customer needs, instead of relying on "by the book" solutions.

Yet the liberal arts cannot claim skills like critical thinking as their exclusive territory. Michael Page, Bentley's former provost and vice president for academic affairs, comments, "As an engineer turned finance academic, I also teach students to think critically. For us, the fusion of arts and sciences and business is about producing responsible citizens capable of thriving in a very dynamic, changing business world and contributing positively to broader society."

It is the dynamism of today's business landscape that explains why business leaders want the whole package—hard and soft skills. The particular pressures of business hiring also explain why they might believe that one set of skills is more valuable, but act as if another set has priority.

In the short term, people are typically hired to satisfy immediate needs. If a business's accounting department is overwhelmed by new work, it looks for qualified accountants to relieve the burden. It can't wait a year for a high-potential math major with great critical thinking skills to get up to speed in accounting.

Business especially needs talented managers. Management requires factual knowledge of the field, and also requires soft skills like communication, seeing the big picture (how one's specialty contributes to the whole), and the capacity to work creatively. Bock commented, "You don't want your Tax Department staffed entirely with people who don't know how to fill out a tax return. But even in those departments, we try to mix in people with different backgrounds and novel thinking."[12]

China Gorman notes another complication. "Business is complicit in the mismatch when they have default job requirements for most jobs. There are a million jobs out there that are going unfilled because employers are requiring a four-year degree when the degree per se is not necessary. If you're looking at call center people, or if you're looking at sales positions, if you're looking at entry level in a lot of business, is a college degree required for that? Job descriptions traditionally are heavy on certification and degree requirement, and light on competencies and experience."

This dynamic tension between short-term demand and long-term development is a never-ending challenge for business leaders. (And it's not limited to hiring, as the relentless focus on short-term financial results testifies.) Moreover, the accelerating rate of change in business worldwide intensifies the challenge.

The Speed of Change

Business needs technical skills of all kinds, and also people with the capacity to change with the times. You can be brilliant at a computer programming language, but when a better system comes along, you have to learn it or quickly become obsolete. Legislation and regulation change the environment for fields like finance and health care. Technical knowledge is valuable in the short term, but a person's ability to learn and apply the latest, best technology is what creates value over the long term. "There is a need to retool yourself, and you should not expect to stop," AT&T chairman Randall Stephenson recently told employees. People who did not spend five to ten hours a week in online learning, he cautioned, "will obsolete themselves with the technology."[13] This kind of continuous learning on the job is a major growth opportunity for MOOC providers like Coursera.[14]

Technical knowledge is valuable in the short term, but a person's ability to learn and apply the latest, best technology is what creates value over the long term.

Industry-wide disruption is a common story today, and the next innovation can rock the most hidebound business. And what will cause disruption is uncertain. Take the example of personal transportation. Twenty years ago, you bought a car, rented a car, or hailed a taxi. In 2000, Zipcar offered an alternative to car ownership by positioning automobiles in urban areas that subscribers could use as needed. In 2008, Tesla introduced its electric car—not the first electric car but one with two disruptive concepts: high performance and design (making it a status symbol) and direct sales (bypassing the need for dealerships and their complex business arrangements with manufacturers). When Tesla announced its lower-cost Model 3 in 2016, it received almost 200,000 preorders in one day (and not incidentally raising $200 million in cash—based on a $1,000 deposit for each order—on that same day). In 2011, Uber and Lyft upended the taxi business by enabling drivers and passengers to bypass traditional regulations. Here's disruption for you: in April 2013, the cost of a taxi medallion in New York City was $1.3 million and had never fallen; two years later, it had dropped 25 percent to $840,000.[15]

In each case, technology was only part of the picture. Opportunity lay also in a vision of disrupting slow-moving, twentieth-century business models. By contrast, the two-wheeled Segway, once hyped as a revolution in personal transportation, remains a novelty. It neither disrupted an existing business nor widely replaced a similar product.

Consider these disruptions in an ordinary, well-known business like personal transportation; multiply that by the thousands of business sectors in the economy and you get an idea of the scale of disruption we could witness. That's what we have to prepare graduates to handle—and indeed, to participate in with enthusiasm.

Rick Miller, president of Olin College, underscores what Daniel Pink and others have suggested: we're moving rapidly from the "knowledge economy" identified by Peter Drucker in the previous century to an "innovation economy."[16] The recent innovations in personal transportation are good examples. Miller defines business innovation as the process of having valuable, original insights (or creations) and then implementing them so they are accepted and used by significant numbers of people.

Olin is an engineering college, so Miller has a keen sense of education from the technical side, but he too suggests that the skills needed in the innovation economy can't be limited to engineering. There's a big disconnect between employers and educators that Olin is trying to repair: the need for technical experts who also have the skills, behaviors, and attitudes that it takes to succeed in today's complex and rapidly changing world. Those attributes include a passion for defining and solving problems, an ability to work on teams and lead teams, effective communication, and broad thinking across disciplines and cultures.

Prepare for the Innovation Economy

Addressing the University of Pennsylvania class of 2009, former Google CEO Eric Schmidt said, "You can't plan innovation or inspiration, but you can be ready for it, and when you see it, you can jump on it."[17] That's quite an assertion from a leader who led the world's most innovative, inspiration-driven, and disruptive company during its fastest growth period.

Google is a prime example of the unpredictability of innovation. Larry Page and Sergey Brin did not set out to create the world's most effective advertising medium. Their first innovation involved changing the ways a search engine ranked web pages, thus delivering a more relevant result to the searcher. In 1999, Google started to sell advertising, using a standard cost-per-thousand (CPM) pricing model, the "eyeballs" model of print and broadcast advertising. After the dot-com implosion of 2000, advertisers scorned the CPM model as ineffective. Online banner advertising, the joke went, was on its way to becoming a "zero-billion-dollar industry."

By 2002, Google created its second great innovation, and it was as much a business model disruption as a clever technology. Google sold ads based on "click-through"; in other words, advertisers paid only when people expressed interest by clicking on a link. This upended the century-old CPM model.

In the twentieth century, John Wannamaker (founder of one of America's first great department stores) quipped that he knew he wasted half his advertising budget, but the trouble was, he didn't know which half. Click-through, a relatively simple technology, was a dramatic change for advertisers because it told them exactly which advertising dollars were well spent. Google destroyed the underlying assumption of advertising, a worldwide business worth $520 billion.[18]

> The technology is terrific, but the *business opportunity* Google discovered was that it could eliminate the biggest flaw in advertising—its reliance on a shotgun approach to reach interested buyers.

In 2001, Google's advertising revenue was $66 million. By 2014, it was $59 billion—growing about 90,000 percent in thirteen years.[19] For all of Google's other innovations, advertising still accounts for 90 percent of revenue. The technology is terrific, but the *business opportunity* Google discovered was that it could eliminate the biggest flaw in advertising—its reliance on a shotgun approach to reach interested buyers.

What else did Google and other innovators like Amazon and Apple do to create new businesses? A quick review shows the interplay of left- and right-brain thinking.

They created new technology, and used technology creatively. This is the most obvious innovation. Internet technologies (first conceived at universities, nonprofits, and government agencies) gave new capabilities to

Amazon, Google, and millions more businesses. They applied fundamental technologies like relational databases in new ways. They created software that rendered discrete new insights from vast amounts of data.

They solved the shortcomings of existing businesses. Google replaced doubt with certainty. Its click-through ad pricing (and many other innovations) took the uncertainty of CPM ad pricing out of the business equation.

They created better stuff. In hindsight this is obvious, but it is also very hard to do. Digital music players in 2000 were difficult to use. Apple's iPod was not only elegant but, when teamed with the iTunes store, offered a seamless, simple way to buy and enjoy music.

They piled on advantages. Amazon's online sales model enabled low pricing, huge inventory, and crowdsourcing reviews (with its star ratings), all advantages over brick-and-mortar stores. In the 1980s, Barnes & Noble clobbered small bookstores with low pricing and inventory, but Amazon's online model could do both better, and star ratings were a breakthrough advantage over limited book reviews or best-seller lists.

They leveraged existing infrastructure to create new business lines. Amazon web hosting (AWS) grew out of the infrastructure first built to support Amazon's online retail business. In 2016, its revenue approached $10 billion.[20] Google's Chrome web browser evolved to become an applications platform (for Google products) and even a laptop operating system. Google Maps evolved to compete with GPS systems on mobile devices.

To Eric Schmidt's point: if innovation or inspiration can't be planned, how can a company survive in the innovation economy?

It's said that the best business leaders recognize opportunity; it's more precise to say that these men and women separate the right opportunities from hundreds of ideas that appear promising but won't succeed. That's the purpose of all the analysis and quantification tools we teach business students to put into business plans. Anyone can come up with a good idea ("Let's make the world's best search engine!"), but it takes just the right application of skills, creativity, capital, analysis, and timing—yes, luck and a few misses are involved along the way—to see that a long-established business model (such as an advertising revenue model) could be replaced with a much more attractive one.

The innovation economy is so associated in the public imagination with technology (more specifically digital technology) that it's easy to think of it as a cascade of shiny new gadgets. But smart watches and electric cars are only a small part of the innovation economy. For example, innovation means reimagining work processes and methods of every kind, from manufacturing to services to transportation to health care to finance to construction. The key to the innovation economy is a drive toward creativity that takes nothing for granted, and the ability to synthesize information and insight from many disciplines. Innovation sees connections not previously made, and opportunities not previously noticed.

But making it happen is not easy. Traditional forces in business hamper innovation. Just one example: much as business leaders admire ideas like creativity, transparency, collaboration, and other aspects of innovation, they inevitably feel the pressure to maximize profits, especially in the short term. Regulation, shareholders, contractual obligations—there's a lot embedded in business that discourages pure innovation. Yet when I talk to business leaders, they all accept the risk of failure. In fact, most believe that risking failure by innovating is the only path to long-term success.

Preparing graduates for the innovation economy . . . means thinking deeply about how changes in technology, business models, and even culture create opportunity in every industry, at every level.

Preparing graduates for the innovation economy requires a shift in thinking about professional skills and attitudes. It means thinking deeply about how changes in technology, business models, and even culture create opportunity in every industry, at every level. And it means training, encouraging, celebrating, *demanding* that kind of thinking—along with risking failure—as part of learning.

Assuming a business is committed to innovation, how does it enable employees to explore and exploit original ideas?

How the Best Cross Boundaries

Laszlo Bock emphasized Google's ironclad rule of hiring: never compromise on quality—for any position in the company, anywhere. That's easy to say but hard to do. The pressure to compromise—to fill seats with "good enough" employees—is enormous. Who can afford the best in every case? What department can wait another week or month to fill a desperately needed position?

Bock's point is that Google is the company it is today *because* they never compromised on quality in hiring, for anyone. Google's unorthodox hiring methods made the biggest difference in selecting the best people. For example, Google always includes a candidate's future subordinates as interviewers, and ranks their opinions as highly as those of senior executives.[21]

The best managers at Google, according to Bock, share attributes in a wide range of those left-brain/right-brain domains. They are technical experts in software engineering (left brain), good communicators and coaches (right brain), results oriented (left brain—results are always quantified), and concerned about others' well-being (right brain).

In short, the highest-rated Google managers straddle the domains of hard and soft skills. They have unique styles and temperaments and strengths, but it's their ability to use both hard and soft skills that makes them standouts even in an elite workforce.

The most familiar example of a business dedicated to merging the domains of left-brain and right-brain thinking is Apple.

It consistently tops *Fortune* magazine's list of most admired companies because it is the exemplar of merging creativity, innovation, and design genius with superb business management. (Apple's current CEO, Tim Cook, trained as an industrial engineer at Auburn, earned an MBA at Duke, and was Apple's operations chief.) You don't produce financial numbers like Apple's without great financial management, and you don't charge premium prices for your gadgets unless they provide a superior experience.

The fusion of left-brain and right-brain thinking is happening all over the innovation economy in companies large and small.

Apple and Google are famous innovators, but again, innovation is not limited to technology. The fusion of left-brain and right-brain thinking is happening all over the innovation economy in companies large and small:

- Human resources recruiters are paying attention. Hiring at innovative companies includes assessing a candidate's emotional intelligence and ability to empathize with customers. *Left brain:* technical skills; *right brain:* emotional intelligence

- Today's most in-demand skill sets are notable for the versatility they require, according to labor market analytics firm Burning Glass.[22] For example, business development requires both strategy and relationship-building skills. *Left brain*: turning data analysis into strategy; *right brain*: relationship building, empathy.

- Dropbox and Box.com, starting as online storage businesses, created drop-dead-simple ways to manage, collaborate, and share documents and files. Then instead of offering a tiny bit of storage for free, they offered immense storage inexpensively. *Left brain:* keeping data safe and available; *right brain:* simple and even elegant interface design.

- Netflix, in the words of *Fast Company,* "turned the TV network into an app." Netflix produced its own shows and then premiered entire seasons at once, popularizing the recreation we call "binge watching." *Left brain:* broadband video delivery; *right brain:* enabling a fun new experience.

- Charles Best of DonorsChoose.org upended traditional fundraising for schools by allowing donors to pick individual classes or projects to support, changing the experience of supporting public education by making each donation personal. *Left brain:* managing dollars donated; *right brain:* creating one-to-one relationships between donors and recipients.

- A host of breakout retailers—Starbucks, Target, Michael Kors, Warby Parker—invented a category called "affordable luxury." *Left brain:* spending money sensibly; *right brain:* satisfying a desire for beauty, style, good taste, and high quality.

Recently, Bentley leveraged labor market analytics from Burning Glass to learn more about today's jobs. When we analyzed the content of thousands of job descriptions, we learned that business is moving into the era of the hybrid job—and the hybrid employee. The successful employee of tomorrow will combine traditional soft skills like communication and collaboration with those hard, technical skills that used to belong to a select tech-savvy group.

> More and more schools are finding creative ways to truly integrate liberal arts strengths with professional and technical skills. It is the way we need to teach and work—by helping develop the ability to view opportunities, challenges, and problems through multiple perspectives, whether the person is a student or an employee.

Businesses of all kinds need people who can cross traditional boundaries, because innovation of all kinds is the key to delivering value in a globalized world. Learning to innovate has to be a foundation of preparing for a career. Fortunately, the ability to innovate *can* be learned, and although much of the higher education community has been slow to realize this, it is an idea taking hold in colleges and universities, especially in the United States. More and more schools are finding creative ways to truly integrate liberal arts strengths with professional and technical skills. It is the way we need to teach and work—by helping develop the ability to view opportunities, challenges, and problems through multiple perspectives, whether the person is a student or an employee. It is exactly the type of change and innovation necessary to drive our economy.

Northeastern University president Joseph Aoun recently wrote in the *Harvard Business Review* that "hybrid jobs call for hybrid education." Aoun recalled his discussions with employers across a range of industries: "They say that the employees who are in highest demand are those who can work in complex teams and think across complex systems. Employers are looking for the sort of professional who can lead a team that includes, for instance, an engineer, a coder, and a data scientist, effectively understanding all the distinct roles and coordinating across them."[23]

Finally, Thomas Friedman and Frank Bruni provided memorable ways to think about the qualities most needed in the job market. With his gift for phrasemaking, Friedman wrote, "The best jobs in the future are going to be what I call STEMpathy jobs—jobs that blend STEM skills (science, technology, engineering, math) with human empathy." He added that we need to "make sure that learning stresses as much of the humanities and human interactive skills as hard sciences."[24] Bruni wrote, "It's impossible to put a dollar value on a nimble, adaptable intellect, which isn't the fruit of any specific course of study and may be the best tool for an economy and a job market that change unpredictably."[25]

The Hybrid Generations

One more factor is driving business to need a new kind of graduate: workplaces across America will soon be staffed by Baby Boomers, Generation Xers, Millennials, and Generation Z. Four generations will be working side by side for the first time since most Americans left the family farm behind. This is going to be interesting.

The cohort currently taking over the new workplace is the Millennials. There are 72 million of them in the United States, and by 2025, they will make up 75 percent of the American workforce. By sheer force of numbers, Millennials will have the same impact on the coming decades as the Baby Boomers had on the decades between 1960 and 2000.

Generation Z has much in common with Millennials, but you might say they're Millennials on steroids. They were children when 9/11 and the Great Recession happened, so they have never known a time of what other generations would call "peace and prosperity." On a personal level, they are highly confident of their abilities, especially with technology. They are the most diverse generation in American history, and on questions about diversity and inclusion they ask, "What's the big deal?" They naturally multitask across many devices—television, computers, and smartphones—and between search engines and apps, they feel resourceful and competent to answer questions. And one of the most powerful forces shaping their lives is social media. They use Facebook, Twitter, Instagram, Snapchat, Slack, Periscope, and all the rest as a primary learning and communications platform, and that has big implications for business and educators.

These are generations that blur lines. They don't see social life and free time as totally separate from work and career. It's all part of one world in their minds, and as they grow in size as part of the workforce, those of us in higher education and business have to understand their ways.[26]

According to the Deloitte 2015 Millennial survey, when deciding where they want to work, nearly 80 percent of

Millennials are influenced by how innovative a company is.[27] Yet most say that their current employer does not greatly encourage them to think creatively.

Millennials in the survey also felt they were stronger on "softer" rather than "technical" skills at graduation. Globally, women in the survey significantly outpolled men when it came to self-assessment of their professionalism, intellectual capabilities, flexibility, communication strategies, and maturity. Men skewed toward greater belief in their analytical, IT, and leadership skills.[28]

The Millennials as a group value innovation and right-brain qualities. They grew up with every form of digital technology and came of age during the rise of social media. They are accustomed to the new normal of business: innovation, globalization, rapid change, and the creative destruction of long-standing business models. Generation Z takes innovation one step further, with a soaring percentage seeing themselves as entrepreneurs: they don't just get jobs; they make them.

In my experience, Millennials and Generation Z are adaptable and open. Such activities as reverse mentoring, in which Millennials share their technical acumen with older generations, are becoming part of the most productive workplaces.

Millennials are the generation that started in college during the last years of the dot-com boom and bust. Their college and early career years also coincided with the rise of globalization. Their ways of learning and working are as different from their predecessors as their technology is different from that of previous generations. They are natural boundary crossers, both geographically and in terms of traditional left-brain/right-brain domains of work. And in the next few years, they are going to begin to fill the ranks of leadership in business and society.

So these generations love innovation, get the model of combining hard and soft skills, and are seamlessly tuned in to connected technology. They're also optimistic and worldly—but they are intolerant of institutions that won't change to address their particular strengths and culture. When I came to Bentley, this above all was clear: it wasn't up to *them* to change to suit an older model of higher education. The question for higher education is how universities and colleges can adapt to them. Their learning, attitudes, and skills will define the economy and culture for decades to come. (I'll say more about the current and next generation of students and employees in chapter 7.)

So business needs a new graduate to power the innovation economy. And for that reason, this generation of students needs a new educational experience to prepare for the world after graduation. In the next chapter, we'll see what that experience must include.

4

STUDENTS NEED A NEW COLLEGE EXPERIENCE

D an Merica, the political producer for CNN mentioned in chapter 1, went to college intending to study international business. In his sophomore year, he switched to communications. Merica says,

> I came to Bentley thinking that I wanted to be a business major, intending to do international business. I always had a passion for foreign relations, understanding foreign countries, and traveling. I went abroad for my entire sophomore year. I studied six months in Australia and six months in France. I wrote for the school newspaper from abroad. I did a lot of journaling and blogging. And it was then that I realized that what I really wanted to do was to be a writer, to be a journalist, to be a reporter.
>
> That ambition was a little out of the box for a Bentley student at the time, and if you had told me at graduation that I'd be doing what I'm doing now, I'd have thought you were crazy. But professors fostered both my love of writing and my love of studying foreign affairs. I consider them as mentors and even as friends.

Transitioning from business to journalism was just the beginning. After graduating Bentley, Merica earned a master's degree in public affairs and journalism at American University. He found his calling by merging business knowledge, journalism skills, and a love of foreign affairs, which eventually carried him from a business school to CNN's political team.

Merica would be the first to tell you that his great formative experience took place *outside* the classroom, weaving together these leadership, journalism, business, and foreign affairs skills he was learning *inside* the classroom. It started with the tragedy of the Haitian earthquake on January 12, 2010.

"I was watching the news on CNN, with all those horrific pictures," he remembers. "And I couldn't help but think this is the kind of thing that students, with their collective brain-power, could help fix. Other students felt the same. I wrote emails to professors, faculty, and staff. They encouraged us, funded us, and we started an initiative called Project Haiti. We did a cross-campus effort to raise money for the effort, involving everyone from the board of trustees to students."

As Bentley's president, I sat in on Merica's project briefings. I was proud and excited to support Project Haiti and its team of students, deans, professors, and staff, first as they planned the initiative and then as they made it a reality. After analyzing different options for action, Project Haiti settled on fundraising for an international disaster relief organization called Shelter Box, which provides an all-in-one shelter kit for disaster survivors.

The student organizers set a goal of raising $30,000 by staging three events that would weave awareness and fundraising into the social life of the school. The signature event, called A Night for Haiti, included live music, comedy, raffles, games, and food—and a period of silence and speeches to recall the earthquake's victims. Slideshows and video presentations helped guests learn more about Haiti before the disaster as well as the struggle to rebuild that survivors would face. A group of campus designers created a banner that members of the community signed, pledging support. (They gave me the honor of kicking it off with my personal pledge to donate a Shelter Box.) To raise money from event attendees, Merica and his team put together a gift package containing a Project Haiti T-shirt and wristband, as well as a CD of music by Bentley student bands. The five hundred packages sold out at $10 each, kicking off a drive that raised $35,000 for Project Haiti in just a few months.

The project continued in the autumn of 2010 with an academic course called the Haiti Relief Project, taught by Shawn Hauserman, then the assistant director of academic programs at the Bentley Service-Learning and Civic Engagement Center.[1]

Hauserman remembers,

> There was a fundraising piece and an academic piece. On the academic side, I taught a consulting class that had a client who was a Bentley alumna, an MBA who was a member of the Haitian diaspora, Rebecca Rosemé Obounou. Her nonprofit organization, Christian Haitian Entrepreneurial Society (CHES), needed to put some systems and structure around what they hoped to accomplish, and so I taught a class in which we did an analysis of how they could increase their capacity and improve their systems to better meet the organization's mission and vision. We were successful on a number of levels. Her organization is still in operation and continuing their work on behalf of the Haitian people ...
>
> I believe in the necessity of a broad and deep understanding of events and circumstances that form the operations of an organization. That meant learning about Haiti's culture and the history, the unique needs of the community as well as CHES's particular needs. The deeper learning for students was to apply the business skills they had acquired to a social purpose. It helped students define what it means to

be a business professional beyond the certification of a CPA or a CFA or an MBA, and to determine the role in society they will play both locally and globally.

Project Haiti was much more than a fundraiser. It embodied the multidimensional experiences students can and should create and receive at today's colleges. Beginning with feelings of compassion for disaster victims, students went beyond a simple fundraising idea. They built a response based on what they were especially qualified to do. They used business skills and creative skills. They analyzed options based on factors like return on investment and transparency. They debated which plan best combined their skills, passions, and beliefs to wrest the most value out of their actions.

Students today need a new college experience, one that brings a renewed emphasis on the soft skills—relationship building, passionate interest, and experiential learning—while at the same time conferring technical mastery and the ability to keep learning far into the future.

This is the kind of educational experience students need today: one that entails acquiring technical skills and applying them immediately in the real world, in the context of students' exploring their role and impact on society. Just as business today needs a new graduate, students today need a new college experience, one that brings a renewed emphasis on the soft skills—relationship building, passionate interest, and experiential learning—while at the same time conferring technical mastery and the ability to keep learning far into the future. Those are the keys to a successful preparation for work and life after graduation.

Improving the College Experience

The question of what constitutes "success" has always been a tempting topic for sociologists, newspaper columnists, and late-night philosophers in college dormitories. I'm not going to settle the question here, but as someone who has spent a decade helping prepare college students for success in career and life, I'll share a commonsense definition: success means achieving happiness, fulfillment, and material security according to one's deeply considered beliefs and values. For some, success means creating a new business, getting rich, and leading thousands of employees in a global enterprise. For others, it means setting up Shelter Boxes as a volunteer in the world's disaster areas.

How can one single college prepare thousands of students with myriad life goals, and set them on a course for the infinite number of journeys they will take? The obvious answer is that one single college—no matter which one you choose—can't do all that alone. Families and communities and cultures play a huge part in determining success. The responsibility of college is to prepare every student to move in the direction of his or her greatest potential. To fulfill that responsibility, higher education creates an overall experience that enables, empowers, and encourages individuals to greater levels of achievement and self-awareness.

Lest that seem a vague promise, consider the complexity of the project: to teach ever-growing bodies of knowledge and ever more complex skills, while at the same time helping young people navigate their own changing preferences and ambitions. It would be far less complex to design a college experience that only conferred mastery of a technical discipline like accounting or supply-chain management, and leave self-discovery to other institutions.

Many colleges are focused on improving the experience of college along these lines, and their newfound focus is producing results. There is no single model that works, and you can fill a bookshelf with thoughtful proposals. (I have one such bookshelf in my office.)

At the University of Michigan's Ross School of Business, a comprehensive, four-year program called MERGE (Multi-disciplinary Exploration & Rigorous Guided Education) begins with a freshman year devoted entirely to liberal arts and sciences. With that as a foundation, subsequent years concentrate on business skills including management and strategy, and also feature study abroad and ways to use business as a tool to improve society.[2]

Olin College of Engineering was founded on the belief that the traditional engineering curriculum is too narrow and technical—as its founders said, "teaching students how to solve problems but not how to find the right problems to solve." Olin weaves hands-on engineering with a curriculum in arts, humanities, social sciences, and entrepreneurship. One of its capstone programs is called Affordable Design and

Entrepreneurship, in which fourth-year students travel to communities around the world to use their engineering and business skills to address problems endemic to poverty.[3]

Bentley sustains an environment in which students prepare for a life that encompasses overlapping circles of career, a personal community, citizenship, and global community. Our expertise happens to be the intersection of business and the arts and sciences. Other colleges like Olin might, for example, offer programs combining engineering and the arts and sciences. Still others will stick with a traditional concentration in one domain, such as law, but broaden the traditional curriculum by considering the role of law in broad social issues like economic inequality. The focus of such colleges might be different, but their common mission is universal: again, to prepare young people at a critical stage for a life of economic, social, and personal well-being. To the extent that graduates succeed in that preparation for work and life, these colleges succeed.

Some measures of success are easy to cite—for example, the long-term financial benefit of a college education. As noted earlier, we know that college graduates are employed at a much higher rate and earn more money over their lifetimes than high school graduates with no college degree.[4] That frequently cited contrast is about the financial benefit of college. We also know that higher earnings correlate overall with better physical health.[5] But what about the other factors—sense of purpose, community ties, and social engagement? What about the sense of well-being that comes from subjective feelings like efficacy, autonomy, or playfulness?

Some schools are looking beyond career placement numbers to measure outcomes that matter just as much as employment. We are asking whether students are leading fulfilling lives, as well as succeeding in careers after graduation.

Some schools are looking beyond career placement numbers to measure outcomes that matter just as much as employment.[6] We are asking whether students are leading fulfilling lives, as well as succeeding in careers after graduation. We are asking, What can we do better to encourage those subjective outcomes?

Personal Support Is Essential

Insights like those in the Gallup-Purdue report, and observations from students and educators, suggest the key college experiences that encourage well-being at school and after graduation. In summary, the most positive undergraduate experience includes personal support, hands-on experience, and deep learning.

The Gallup-Purdue report should be studied by anyone contemplating how to improve the student experience. (The report can be found at the Lumina Foundation, which funded the study.[7]) Here again is the list of six factors in the undergraduate experience that made a measureable difference in students' well-being after college:

· A professor who made them excited about learning

- Professors who cared about them as a person
- A mentor who encouraged them to pursue their goals and dreams
- Work on a project that took a semester or more to complete
- An internship that allowed for applying what they were learning in the classroom
- Participation in extracurricular activities and organizations in college

I've talked to many graduates who today are thriving in the workplace, and they all credit one, two, or more of these factors with preparing them for success. The study found that the size or type of school (public or private, selective or nonselective, type of degrees granted) didn't make much of a difference in the overall outcomes. What mattered was the subjective experience each individual had in school, and his or her reaction to that experience.

The study confirmed commonsense truths about higher education that can be lost in the details of debating how best to prepare students for work and life after graduation. People do well when they are simultaneously supported and challenged. Authority in the form of professors, staff, and coaches is important, and so is acceptance in terms of one's cohort. Hands-on learning on complex projects develops habits in a student that will pay off in the world of work. And sustained relationships, in which people authentically care for one another, are the foundation of confidence and growth.

Let's examine how those factors support a stronger learning experience.

Getting Excited about Learning

Most graduates remember teachers whose excitement about their subject was contagious. Students who catch that passion become lifelong learners. In the case of Will Markow, the experience was life changing.

Markow works as a manager of client strategy and client analytics at labor analytics firm Burning Glass Technologies. He majored in managerial economics with a concentration in quantitative analysis, and minored in natural and applied science. A congenital nerd? Hardly:

> My background was a little sordid. My career plan before college was to become a professional boxer. My high school record was anything but sublime, and I ended up going to community college and then transferred to Bentley on the advice of some alums. I eventually realized that hey, learning is kind of fun! It was there that professors, especially the arts and sciences professors, helped me realize just how much I enjoyed using my brain for something other than a punching bag.
>
> I took part in a number of other extracurricular activities on campus that I think also contributed significantly [to my success]. I held a number of different research positions in the science department, I worked at the writing center, and was on the moot court team. The moot court experience was terrific preparation for a lot of the public speaking that I do now. I recently appeared on a radio show, and the whole time I was getting asked questions, all I could think about was how similar it was to being in front of a judge in a moot court competition.

Today, Markow returns the favor professors did him when they unlocked his love of learning. He participates in career center events to encourage students to seek and pursue intellectual passions wherever they lead, and to be willing as he was to change their self-image.

> It's one thing to be told lifelong learners are statistically more likely to be successful and happy and quite another to experience that passionate desire to learn in oneself.

The love of learning is frequently cited as a benefit of higher education, but it isn't enough to witness professors in lecture halls expounding on their knowledge. Markow was told that learning is valuable regardless of one's class or economic status or even intellectual background. Professors and others in his college community gave students permission to be curious, to pursue their passions and become self-starters. It's one thing to be told lifelong learners are statistically more likely to be successful and happy and quite another to experience that passionate desire to learn in oneself. For some, it's all the motivation they need.

Erik Larsson works as a research assistant at the Federal Reserve Board in Washington DC. He grew up in a small town in Massachusetts, and decided to attend the University of Michigan to try college at a big school. "I had an overall positive experience there," he says, "but quickly realized I wasn't adapting to sitting with hundreds of other kids in a big auditorium, listening to a lecturer rather than a full PhD professor. It was a very impersonal feel, and I didn't work too well under that environment.

"I transferred to Bentley in the fall of 2010. For me, you just can't beat a situation where the professor knows you by name and you can actually go to their office hours, and they're excited to see all the students coming to visit them."

Larsson's teachers were distinguished academics and practitioners like David Peter Simon, who had worked at the Federal Reserve, and Claude Cicchetti, a lecturer who develops innovative currency trading strategies. Larsson says, "To get one-on-one time with these extremely talented professors was the biggest difference between my experiences at Michigan and Bentley. There was no weeding-out process in really hard classes. Every professor I ever had actually wanted me to succeed."

Although I understand why they are conducted this way, the introductory course taught in a vast lecture hall might be the college experience most threatened by online technology. The reasons go beyond the convenience and efficiency of online courses; they have to do with the power of human connections as a teacher and student establish a relationship. A professor can't give personal attention to three hundred individuals in a lecture hall, or be invested in their success except in a generalized way.

Gallup's findings confirm that relationships in which teachers can show genuine care and attention to individual students have positive outcomes. A bit of personalized instruction might be part of that, but I believe the reasons go deeper. A teacher's sincere regard for a student encourages that student's self-confidence and sense of value. He or she becomes more willing to take risks, seek creative solutions, and develop other intangible qualities that make the difference between success and mediocrity today, in business and in life.

Mentors and Sponsors

Kristen Steele attended Ohio Northern University, where she majored in professional writing and minored in business administration. There, an internship and a mentor changed her life.

> Going into the end of my sophomore year, I had no idea how to land the required internship, much less what I actually wanted to do for a living when I graduated. My academic advisor introduced me to José Nogueras, the associate director of news services in Ohio Northern University's communications and marketing office. My advisor told him I was a writer with potential, needed an internship, and was clueless about my career path.
>
> Almost on the spot, I was offered a summer internship with ONU's communications and marketing office with José as my mentor. I spent the summer shadowing José in dealing with the news media, making campus "rounds" with José to find out what professors/departments/classes were doing that could potentially be newsworthy, and writing and editing for the university's alumni magazine. I had no idea what I was getting myself into, but soon, I was loving every minute of it. Within a few weeks, I knew marketing and public relations were what I was meant to do.
>
> I maintained that internship until the day I graduated. Not only did I learn the basic tasks that I was told I would, but I learned many more valuable business and life lessons— how to manage people's difficult/stubborn/unreasonable expectations, how to graciously accept criticism, and how not to settle for mediocrity in my work.

The experience and the mentor set Kristen's professional course. Today she's director of marketing and publisher relations for Bookmasters, a book manufacturing and publisher services company in Ashland, Ohio.

In my original profession of law, graduates going to big law firms served a kind of apprenticeship. You might work like a maniac, but somebody was mentoring you. This someone could be a benevolent person regularly offering encouragement, or an incredibly tough curmudgeon.

Either way, you weren't alone. As was the case in law school, there was an active back-and-forth relationship, testing young lawyers with the legal profession's version of the Socratic method. Mentors would look at what the young lawyer had produced and demand, "What do you mean by this statement? Are you sure your research has gone far enough? Why do you make that assumption?" Mentors took young law graduates through a rigorous, iterative process, which generations of lawyers have experienced in order to learn how to get it right. The same thing is true for most postgraduate medical students; internships and residencies are famously hard, not just physically but because someone is watching you, questioning you, and ideally getting you to think more broadly about what you're doing.

I was fortunate enough to have a strong and supportive mentor/sponsor during my time at the Federal Trade Commission. Commissioner Patricia Bailey saw my potential and actively took me under her wing. During our time working together, Pat challenged me and helped guide me through the political world of the 1980s. Pat was a female presidential appointee, no small feat in Washington DC at that time, and I worked hard to learn everything I could from her every day. Although our work styles were different, we complemented each other, and my approach to my post at Bentley today reflects much of what I learned from Pat.

Organizational researchers advise people in business or college to find mentors who can offer advice, give insight into the organization, and provide an objective sounding board for ideas or problems. In schools, mentors are frequently the teachers I just described, who care about students, share their passion for learning, and offer advice.

In appropriate circumstances, I like to raise the expectations for that role by using the term *sponsor* rather than mentor. A sponsor takes a more active role than a mentor in promoting his or her protégé's success. For example, a sponsor will suggest a young professional for a highly visible project, put him or her forward for "stretch" assignments, and secure approval for that person's professional training. Sponsors might alert their protégés to hidden dangers like an unspoken problem with a colleague, or they might suggest connecting with one of an organization's hidden influencers.

Writing in *Fast Company*, Sava Berhané, chief operating officer of the nonprofit Building Excellent Schools, observed that the key difference between a mentor and a sponsor is career capital—that is, "a direct ability to give you opportunities, not just advice about how to maximize them when they come along ... Unlike a mentor, a sponsor is someone who can not only advise you on your career, but actively advance it."[8]

Sometimes the mentor or sponsor appears in the community. The famous financial advice expert Suze Orman tells an amazing story of this kind. She was twenty-nine years old and working as a waitress making about $400 a month. She was determined to open her own restaurant, but neither she nor her parents could come up with the $20,000 investment required in those days. A longtime customer of hers, Fred Hasbrook, discovered her difficulty one morning. Orman remembers, "Fred ate his breakfast and then talked to some of the other customers I'd been waiting on all those years. Before he left the restaurant, he came up to the counter and handed me a personal check for $2,000, a bunch of other checks and commitments from the other customers that totaled $50,000, and a note that read: THIS IS FOR PEOPLE LIKE YOU, SO THAT YOUR DREAMS CAN COME TRUE. TO BE PAID BACK IN TEN YEARS, IF YOU CAN, WITH NO INTEREST. I couldn't believe my eyes."

This wonderful tale might be simply a charming example of someone "paying it forward," but for the multiplier effect of those customers' support. Hasbrook advised Orman to invest the money and open a restaurant with the proceeds. Orman's interest in things financial was piqued, one thing led to another ... and an act of generosity and mentorship initiated a completely different business, as she became a trusted and popular financial advisor to uncounted numbers of her fans globally.[9]

The mentor or sponsor relationship isn't always rainbows and unicorns. Katie Callaghan, who attended Loras College in Dubuque, Iowa, on a swimming scholarship, was surprised by the advice she received. She remembers,

I asked my advisor how to start applying for jobs. And he made me write a list of anything and everything I wanted to do in the future in terms of career goals, life goals, everything. And then he told me to write a list of my top places I wanted to work, where I wanted to live, everything. And then he told me to find open job postings there. He said, "Dream as big as you want, whatever it is." I brought him that homework and … he told me to rip it up in front of him! He said, "You don't know. You have no idea. You're a junior in college. You're twenty years old. Whatever you feel right now is going to totally change in a year, and it's going to change."

He said, "When you're on job interviews you'll know. When they start describing your role or the position, and it sparks something inside you, that's when you'll know what you want to do with it."

That was powerful advice for someone who had hoped to map out a definitive plan at an early age.

Mentoring and sponsoring complement each other. A sponsor might be more role model than counselor; perhaps she doesn't have the more intimate, confiding role or even a fully comfortable relationship with her protégé, but she believes in that person's potential and pushes the protégé to succeed. Sponsors often choose you (rather than you choosing them) and help you chart a successful course.

Betsy Myers, founding director of Bentley's Center for Women and Business and author of *Take the Lead*, said that leading companies take sponsorship very seriously: "When you have a full sponsorship program, the person who's the sponsor has agreed to be your champion. That would mean promoting you and also representing you. A sponsor will give you open and courageous feedback. She'll keep her ears open for you so when somebody says, 'Wow, [that protégé] really doesn't know what she's doing,' the sponsor will say, 'No, no, I think you're off about that.' Or even better, the sponsor will get her protégé and that critic into a room so they can have a really difficult conversation."

Colleges have long assigned mentors to students in various forms and roles, such as thesis advisor or resident advisor. These relationships are a fantastic first resource for students, but those searching for greater and more meaningful opportunities will be best served by seeking out and asking for help from other potential mentors and sponsors, beyond those originally assigned. Jeffrey Selingo, formerly of the *Chronicle of Higher Education* and author of *There IS Life after College*, argued that it's incumbent on students to make this happen. He said, "College graduates who thrive in their careers are the ones who are willing to find professors or mentors to guide them. They begin to build their professional networks in college, and they develop soft skills that employers want. They proactively take on work beyond the rigidity of a syllabus and seek out additional opportunities to learn."[10] In short, students who practice *finding and using* several mentors and sponsors acquire a habit that will serve them well throughout their careers.

> Students who practice *finding and using* several mentors and sponsors acquire a habit that will serve them well throughout their careers.

When a professor truly cares about a student as an individual, the relationship goes well beyond strengthening a student's intellectual engagement. It truly changes her life.

This happened to Laken Brooks, who tells her story of a girl starting out with the odds against her, and ultimately triumphing, because of one professor:

> While studying at Emory & Henry College, a liberal arts school in Virginia, I felt incredibly inadequate. I was stifled by the constant pressure to prove myself to my new honors colleagues and my rural family who had never had a member attend college.
>
> My mentor was my honors program director, Dr. Joseph Lane. His support guided me toward greater self-confidence while also helping me realize my own academic and personal potential. When I wrote my first essay for this professor, he returned it with the phrase "This paper is disappointing. You can do better" typed in red ink. In person, he explained that he knew that I had to work harder than many of the other students because of my background and my family's suspicion of higher education; however, he knew that I was smart enough to overcome my own hesitation. "After I told you to write better, you did," he said. "I would not have given you that feedback unless I knew that you would take it and use it to your benefit."
>
> On my college campus, I was encouraged to abandon my Appalachian accent in favor of a more "academic" dialect. "People will think that you are stupid when they hear you speak," I was oftentimes told. Dr. Lane shook his head sagely when I told him of my attempts to change my voice. "Never be ashamed of where you come from and what brought you here," he said. "Your voice is your tool to share your mind with the world. It is valuable. Do not silence it."
>
> The next year, I heard from another professor that Dr. Lane had been born and raised very near my own home-town; his only path to higher education was with a scholarship. In college at Harvard, he had made every effort to strip himself of his Appalachian identity. He trained himself

to speak in a crisp, Northern tone. Even after returning to his agrarian hometown to teach, he had rid his tongue of all traces of its drawl.

Dr. Lane's family became my support system. I babysat his children and attended conferences with him. When I was a junior, he asked me which graduate schools I might want to attend. I laughed. "I am amazed that I was able to come to college, really. I never thought of grad school. Really, I don't think that I am smart enough. People who go to grad school are so capable." He tilted his head and said. "And you think that you are not? I have never had a student like you, Ms. Brooks. Do not underestimate yourself. Come meet with me next week and tell me when you plan to take the GRE."

Later that year, he called me into his office. "I have nominated you for the Virginia student of the year award," he said. "I do not want you to be disappointed if you do not receive it, but I want you to know that you are incredibly deserving." When I received the notification that I was the recipient, I messaged him to celebrate. He replied, "We will gather some of your classmates and all go to listen to your acceptance speech."

Brooks added this final note when telling her story: "I will always be grateful that Dr. Lane encouraged me to retain my love of literature and of my Appalachian roots, all while instilling within me a love for my own unique voice and an appreciation for myself."

That was the influence of one mentor on one student.

The Critical Cohort

A student's relationships in his cohort of peers are just as important to success as his relationships with teachers. Students spend a lot more time with fellow students than they spend with professors or mentors. Peers in a cohort are more than friends; they are the college equivalent of colleagues and team members later in life.

The college cohort anticipates a trend in the working world. Today, as business settings become more flexible and project oriented, they become a bit more like college and graduate school settings. Virtual work teams set up for a while, contribute their expertise to a new project or program, and collaborate on business goals, sometimes without ever meeting face-to-face. Then they might disband and scatter to form different teams. That's a lot like the semester-by-semester and class-by-class pace of college.

The trend of changing jobs frequently is also making the tempo of work more like that of the college or graduate school experience. Now, instead of working with the same people in the same company for thirty years, the typical first-time employee will spend about four-and-a-half years with an employer and then move on.[11] Employees have a far better ability than ever before to keep in touch after leaving a company, thanks to social and professional networks. Today, LinkedIn and private networks are the Internet-powered version of the venerable college alumni society. A LinkedIn permission-only group for General Electric alumni has more than thirty-six thousand members engaged in hundreds of discussions. A similar group for alumni of the University of Virginia has more than thirty-four thousand members, and even a medium-sized school like Bentley has eighteen thousand members in its group. When it comes to maintaining relationships over time, people are mixing their professional and academic networks.[12]

Research tells us that people are capable of keeping about 150 close relationships going at one time, knowing each person and how that person relates to all the others (a phenomenon called Dunbar's number, after British scholar Robin Dunbar). Beyond that number, relationships become more tenuous. Still, the broad and loose relationships of a large college cohort constitute a pool of potential close relationships for learning or work. The skill of quickly getting to work with near-strangers is appropriate for college to teach, because it's the way work gets done in so many occupations these days. And the ability to create one's own "virtual team" of professional acquaintances is a distinguishing skill of entrepreneurs.

To exercise this important skill early on, colleges should require students to set up temporary teams—and even deliberately prescribe teams comprising members of different backgrounds, temperaments, and skills—to develop the skills demanded by a more mobile workforce. For that matter, learning how to quickly become effective when working with strangers has benefits that go beyond the workplace. Could practicing teamwork in the cohort prepare students for a life of geographic mobility as well? Might it help make communities more cohesive even in a society where people move around in their early working years? Might learning to create beneficial connections overcome some of the alienation and partisanship of today's society? Maybe that's overly optimistic, but if colleges consciously developed that capacity in each student, they'd be fulfilling their purpose of nurturing good citizens.

Experiential Learning

There's a truism in most fields that "you have to *do* it [finance, engineering, accounting, music ...] in order to *learn* it."

Experiential learning—learning by doing, by trying, succeeding and failing, and trying again—is essential to both left-brain and right-brain skill sets. As the Gallup-Purdue study notes, the power of experiential learning is magnified when undergraduates take on long-term projects that apply the skills and knowledge they've learned in the classroom.

> The power of experiential learning is magnified when undergraduates take on long-term projects that apply the skills and knowledge they've learned in the classroom.

Nicole Erhartic, a 2008 Bentley graduate, is today a senior actuary at insurance company Liberty Mutual, and she credits her honors capstone—a full semester-long project—with providing hands-on experiential learning that has helped her career long after her college studies ended.

"We were working for the Massachusetts state government as consultants on energy prices in the state. They told us the kind of help they wanted, but had no specific questions. That's a real-world framework for a problem. Instead of 'Do X, Y, and Z,' they challenged us with, 'Here's a problem that we're having; dig into this industry and find a way to solve it.'

Erhartic also describes how long-term projects, which typically don't have predetermined answers, prepared her for work after graduation. "In the actuarial profession, you might have five different actuaries who would come up with five different answers to determining loss reserves. It's a forecast, not a definite answer. You have to learn to say, 'I know what I know, and I know how to put into practice some techniques to get to an answer, and I know the questions I'm going to be asked and how I'm going to have to defend this answer. I know how to be comfortable with ambiguity.'"

Just like the real world—learning by doing. Academic knowledge confers the foundational information and skills, and then experience builds skills and competence. The more an education can adopt this path to mastery, the better prepared graduates will be for managing their careers after college. Nowhere is this more true than in the internship experience.

Jonathan White, director of the Bentley Service-Learning and Civic Engagement Center, contends that work in the community is a foundation of experiential learning as well. White is internationally known (and honored) for his work connecting the classroom with the real world in the form of for-credit service performed by students, whether that is teaching computer skills to young people in the local community, solving the financial challenges of local organizations, or other acts of civic partnership with the community.

White says, "Service-learning is a pedagogy that is practiced and studied nationally. In Bentley's service-learning model, students are working twenty to twenty-five hours out in the community. They receive about five hours of training from us before their service component; and during and after their service, they write and discuss reflections that connect it back to the academic components [such as computer skills or finance in the previous examples]. It's the most effective academic pedagogy of all the experiential learnings in terms of outcomes. Everything from social and cultural outcomes to academic outcomes to student-faculty interaction to alumni giving." (I'll describe service-learning in more detail in chapter 6.)

The Modern Internship

Well-designed internships give undergraduates great preparation for the world of work. This is common knowledge in college business programs, but only recently has it become obvious that every student, in every major, should step into internships while in college. Before the Great Recession, a lot of young people had summer jobs unrelated to work. They assumed they were still going to get a great job after graduation if they kept their grades up, so a summer spent doing a job unrelated to future career was fine. But now well-designed internships are "the new first job," especially as expectations for the skill level of graduates climb.[13]

"Well-designed" is the hard part of making internships count. The work should be more than C-level administrative tasks. It should include real decision making, working with an engaged manager who has the time and training to develop the intern as if he or she were a new full-time employee. The best internships include regular contact with a mentor who can explain company culture and put work in the context of the big picture. For example, an intern can attend meetings with executives, and later debrief with a manager on how his or her department's work contributes in detail to long-term strategy. In a hands-on internship, students can wrestle with business realities like budget and time constraints, or learn how success will be measured in a particular job.

Both colleges and businesses acknowledge that they need to work more closely together to make internships connect academic learning and real-world practice. That means

> Businesspeople have to spend more time on campus in career centers and classrooms, talking about their particular needs.

businesspeople have to spend more time on campus in career centers and classrooms, talking about their particular needs. They need to tell students how certain skills are applied, why company culture matters, and which skills and abilities they value most. They need to regard internships as early job interviews, not as cheap labor. Business has long done this with MBA summer associates, but that long-term preparation is now important to hiring those who have just earned undergraduate degrees. Karen Kaplan, chairman and CEO of advertising firm Hill Holliday, says, "The ramp-up has to be much longer than the abrupt graduation model. We at Hill Holliday participate in classes, guest lectures, [and as] competition judges, and work with undergraduates to give students a clearer understanding of what advertising is about, what Hill Holliday's culture is about … We have about one hundred interns a year come through, hiring about 15 percent. We have a specialized internship for postgraduates in creative work, and end up hiring about 50 percent of those."

Internships matter as much to liberal arts graduates as to business graduates. Liberal arts programs should get close to businesses in their communities and redouble their efforts to bring alumni back to campus to design relevant internships with the career centers and to recruit undergraduates. For the liberal arts undergraduate, an internship can open a nonobvious career path. Alumni who majored in biology and went on to work in marketing, or who majored in communications and now apply those skills in a government office or construction firm, might be especially valuable internship sponsors.

It's also incumbent on today's graduates to be strategic about the type of internship they want, and to customize their internship if it is possible to do so. That means building an active partnership with the college career office and influential professors as early as freshman year. The earlier that students think about how lessons they're learning in the classroom match internship opportunities, and the more they show up in the career office and test those ideas in an active internship program, the better their internship experiences will be.[14]

Insurance giant Liberty Mutual uses internships to identify potential long-term employees. In a study of its interns, the company found that they had a greater retention rate, more diverse representation, and more competitive performance ratings as a group than nonintern college hires.[15] Matt Venus, who earned an MBA at Bentley in 2013, represents that kind of success. He first encountered the company as an intern in 2006, when he was a rising senior undergraduate at Bentley. Venus worked in the affinity marketing group that summer and was hired by Liberty Mutual's technology group the following year. He has since moved around the company, working in finance within personal insurance and finally returning to information systems. Now he is a business systems analyst and consultant to many internal groups, helping the company adopt a lean management model.

The fact that internships are time limited and meant for exploration can inspire students, if they are willing, to try work that they might otherwise consider too risky for a long-term career.

The fact that internships are time limited and meant for exploration can inspire students, if they are willing, to try work that they might otherwise consider too risky for a long-term career. A media major might spend a semester or a summer working in the web development group of a bank, and discover to her surprise that some of the most interesting online design problems are found in a business where huge data sets must coexist with user-friendly interfaces.

Finally, good internships drive home the necessity of acquiring practical skills. In this day and age, you can't expect to coast into a job armed only with a good GPA at a good school. Ian Cross, professor of marketing and director of the Center for Marketing Technology at Bentley, sums it up perfectly:

> It's a false promise often foisted on students that the prestige of their alma mater will compensate for their lack of practical knowledge and ability. Especially in a digital economy, what a student knows and has done is far more important than where the student went to school, what he or she majored in, or even their grade-point average. The question every student today needs to ask is, "What should I do to

be relevant?" That applies not only inside the classroom but outside it as well, especially when it comes to internships. Colleges and students need to insist that internships include exposure to cutting-edge practices. Otherwise, students are largely wasting their time.

The Cocurricular Experience

Extracurricular activities at their best help students learn more about themselves, develop qualities like empathy and skills like teamwork, and express their values. Whether an activity is a service project, a sport, or a club, we call it "cocurricular" at Bentley, because we believe that these activities complete the curriculum by developing a whole person. Cocurricular activities inspire self-knowledge. And let's not forget the importance of having a little fun!

Do cocurricular activities contribute to the qualities that promote success at work and life after graduation? What does singing in an a cappella group or volunteering to teach English as a second language classes in the local community have to do with most careers? The answer depends on how much participants consciously relate what they do outside of their studies to the choices they will make later. And people aren't born knowing how to do that—they need the trust and guidance of teachers, mentors, parents, and peers in a continuous conversation.

Dr. J. Andrew Shepardson is Bentley's vice president for student affairs and dean of students. He points out that undergraduates' cocurricular experience teaches them their strengths and weaknesses as part of preparation for the world of work:

> Let's say you've just become the president of a student organization. How do you lead? How do you take a good idea and make it a reality? That's called management.
>
> You soon realize it is not going well. In college, unlike the real world sometimes, you're not doing it on your own; you're meeting with an advisor, a faculty or staff member who can say, "Okay, so you're really struggling with managing people. You're a good, independent worker; should we discuss the fact you're a management major? Does that worry you? If this is a real struggle and you keep reporting you don't like working with people, maybe we can find something you're passionate about doing." An undergraduate will learn a lot from that conversation.
>
> Or the treasurer of a student organization might hear, "You're really good at managing people, and you have great big ideas, but you haven't balanced the books yet and you're an accounting major." This is a rich opportunity! It might lead to a conversation in which the unhappy treasurer admits, "Well, my parents are both accountants, so I think I should be an accountant." And continues with the mentor saying, "Well, okay, but let's talk about who you want to be. What are your future endeavors? What are your strengths, and what inspires you? What about this experience tells you where you might be happy at work?"

The kind of dialogue Shepardson describes can spring up from experiences in athletics, clubs, service organizations, interest groups, travel—all the cocurricular opportunities that can be taken at college with great variety to experiment. It can take place with a greater margin of psychological safety in a college environment than in other situations, such as a family business. It can teach people how to succeed with humility or fail gracefully. It can allow someone to commit to a project for the purpose of self-discovery and, based on that self-knowledge, commit even more or decide that it's not right for him or her.

Conversations that raise awareness of a student's strengths and weaknesses can happen in a mentor's office, in a residence hall, or with an engaged alumnus like Dan Merica or Will Markow or Nicole Erhartic. But most students don't arrive on campus knowing they should have those conversations. The cocurricular experience offers a rich environment to gain insight about oneself because it can encourage those conversations.

This is one of the big contrasts I've seen between today's generation of students and previous generations: with so many choices and so much at stake, today's students need a more deliberate, individual experience than might have been important in previous generations. Yes, many in my generation questioned the system, and there was plenty of debate about the value of certain knowledge (for example, those required reading lists that hadn't changed in twenty years). But beyond the content of the courses, we had fewer choices. Our lives were more compartmentalized; you had class work, you had extracurricular activities, and you had time off. We didn't see those college years as a fully integrated, interdependent preparation for work and life.

It's natural that today's students should regard cocurricular experience and classroom experience as connected and integrated, because that's how they experience the world.

Today's students assume that the stakes of their decisions are higher, in part because of the cost of college, but also because they have a less compartmentalized mind-set.

Millennials and Gen Z don't see dividing lines separating work and play, or separating achievement in their studies and achievement in cocurricular activities. The Internet and social media and 24/7 information and even these students' global orientation encourage a sense of everything blending together in a flow or personal narrative of experience. It's natural that today's students should regard cocurricular experience and classroom experience as connected and integrated, because that's how they experience the world.

Choosing Their Own Path

As today's students choose their own path, there are new questions for them to ask before they decide on which college to attend, and also during their college years. I've listed some of the most important questions here. Returning to these questions periodically, with the support of faculty and staff, students can help create an experience more in tune with today's economic realities than the experience of older generations.

Is the curriculum relevant to my goals?   Few undergraduates can predict where they will work five or ten years from today, even if they are very directed in their interests, and strong preparation means acquiring a broad set of intellectual skills. Can you have more than one major, and in different disciplines? Will you combine the left-brain and right-brain domains, or hard and soft skills described in chapter 3? How will you integrate those skills? How will you learn to communicate what you know? Will you need to learn how to persuade people to your point of view? Will you learn to defend your ideas?

What's the role of technology in my learning?   There are three important questions about technology in the college setting: Will you learn the specific technologies required by your field and the areas that interest you most? How is technology used in the classroom—merely as an information-delivery platform or to do original work? Will you learn both hands-on skills and the more generalized intellectual skills to apply new technologies to work years from now?

What will cocurricular life be like?   There's wisdom in the observation that you will be as influenced by your peers as by your professors. Are there classmates who share your passionate interests, values, and ambitions? What are the popular student groups, sports, and opportunities for on- and off-campus civic engagement? How comfortable are you with the size of the student population and the nature of the surrounding community? What do people do on weekends?

What will best prepare me for life after college?   How best to prepare for life after college is the central question of this book. There isn't a single answer, but all the elements I've cited from the Gallup-Purdue Index and Bentley's PreparedU project are part of each individual's answer. Give special scrutiny to the design and funding of internships I've described and to the quality of a college's career office. Is career study part of college life from the first days at school? Is the office adequately staffed, in tune with today's changing economy? What are its relationships with companies and organizations that might hire you, or with alumni who might offer insights and networking opportunities?

How does the college culture fit into the big picture of my life? Asking this question begs the other big questions: What do I value? What for me describes social, financial, physical, and personal well-being? Do I believe that college is ultimately about preparing for career alone or for having a larger personal vision?

Today, many leading companies are turning from a single-minded emphasis on profit to the point of view described as the triple bottom line: profit–people–planet. They see their role not simply as creators of wealth for shareholders but also as social actors, changing the world for the better.

Many of today's students are doing much the same. They are looking for a triple bottom line in their education. They want to acquire left-brain and right-brain skills that will make them strong economic players; they want to serve others and support their civic values while they are students (and beyond); they seek ways to harmonize economic growth, social good, and global sustainability. I'll say more about the specifics of these attitudes, along with the data that back up my conclusions, in chapter 7.

My question to students considering where to go to college—and *how* to go to college, is this: What's *your* triple bottom line?

5

THE CASE FOR PLACE-BASED EDUCATION

When you are an overachieving student at a top university, you don't expect your academic advisor to suggest time off, but that's what happened to Stephanie Shyu.

I was entering my junior year at Duke, and I had struggled in my first couple of years. I had been a classic overachieving high school student and let it go in my first and second years of college. I was a public policy major with a minor in journalism and media study, but I just couldn't find my stride.

I was supposed to go study abroad in Scotland for junior year. I toyed with the idea of taking a working semester away from campus instead of studying abroad, and applied for an internship at CNN. My academic advisor, professor Ken Rogerson, encouraged me to take a semester off and try the career path I'd never experienced. I got the CNN internship, and Professor Rogerson worked through all the practical matters—making sure I had all my credits lined up to graduate on time ...

I don't think I would have pursued the journalism course without that experience at CNN. I had planned to go to law school, but that semester taught me I could focus more on journalism and media in my later career at Duke. I took unusual courses like Islam in the Media.

With Professor Rogerson's support, Shyu continued on a nontraditional path. She worked in journalism and then decided that law school would supplement her journalism career. Shyu graduated from the University of Pennsylvania Law School in 2014, but pivoted once again to become an entrepreneur. Today she's the founder of a college admissions tech start-up called AdmitSee.com. Without the contrarian advice of Professor Rogerson, Shyu might not have found the courage to take the road less traveled. In 2015, she was named to *Forbes* magazine's prestigious "30 under 30" list. That's the difference one professor, working closely with one student, can make.

> Place-based education—the campus—is a field on which students, professors, mentors, peers, settings, and activities come together to foster a growth experience uniquely suited to that time in life when young people are largely becoming who they will be for decades to come.

Here's what I love about place-based education: even on a single campus, it's a different version of college for each person, because the permutations and combinations of experience are infinite. If you can attend college on a campus, the totality of your personal experience is much richer than it would be if you only spent time in classrooms and then went home. Place-based education—the campus—is a field on which students, professors, mentors, peers, settings, and activities come together to foster a growth experience uniquely suited to that time in life when young people are largely becoming who they will be for decades to come.

Class time and study time are the intellectual center of the college experience, but there is so much more that can, and does, shape a person beyond the classroom. I was a serious student and I loved the classroom, but I also loved the dorm conversations at 2 a.m. I loved discussing what we were studying and the issues of the time, over meals in the dining halls, in residence hall living rooms, and sometimes in stage whispers in the library. Discussions about the antiwar movement, the women's movement, and civil rights were as important as our classroom learning in forming who my peers and I became. And it's happening today on campuses in spontaneous moments when young people apply their intelligence and passion to questions of the day or participate in extracurricular activities or athletics. They are in a very special community that enables them to take risks in those conversations and explore their passions. Perhaps today's especially divisive issues around race, religion, and politics bring even greater import to these campus opportunities.

I'll hasten to add that a place-based education is a privilege. Not everybody can live on a campus for four years, whether because of financial circumstances or commitments to work or family. The higher education system offers off-campus students a range of options, including part-time study and financial aid, as well as online learning. Policymakers are putting forward new options to make college more widely available and affordable. Without prejudice against the alternatives, this chapter will state the case for place-based education.

Will Online Learning Replace the Campus?

First, a word about the fastest-growing innovation. Every week or so people ask me, "What about online learning?" They're talking about the recent emergence of MOOCs from organizations like edX and Coursera. MOOCs are part of the innovation economy—innovating in education. They are growing in popularity, especially among adults seeking to advance their careers with specialized skills like computer coding. For-profit businesses like Coursera are bringing college-developed courses to business. They have the cost advantage of many Internet-based businesses in terms of delivering an education "product" remotely and less expensively than the brick-and-mortar alternative, the college campus.

MOOCs are changing and progressively becoming part of the education options open to people from all walks of life, and that's a good thing. Their presence makes greater experimentation possible. In course design, they encourage left-brain/right-brain teamwork—for example, helping history courses borrow from information design principles.[1] They cannot, however, fully and adequately replicate a place-based experience. The discussion here is not whether they will replace place-based education but rather what a place-based education offers that no alternative can replicate.

Jonathan White, director of the Bentley Service-Learning and Civic Engagement Center, summarizes the current state of online versus place-based education. I love his passionate approach, so before we look at the advantages of a campus experience, here's his description of the difference:

> I believe in online education; parts of it are really good and bring good benefits. But when I am in a classroom, I can tell

if my students are getting things. I can speak to them right after class. I can know if they're depressed, or for that matter if they're inspired. I can take a walk with a student and say, "Hey, come talk to me about your paper." You can argue with me until you're blue in the face that you can have great faculty-student interaction online. You can tell me that students and teachers can even see each other and talk to each other one-to-one. And while you'd be right, let's be honest that the experience is different; the subtlety of human contact suffers.

The Learning Process and the Growing Process

Andrew Shepardson, Bentley's vice president for student affairs and dean of students, notes that the arc of student life combines a maturation process along with the acquiring of skills and knowledge.

When you're a first-year student, your cognitive development is pretty dualistic. You say, "Give me the rules and I'll follow the rules." You have a hard time figuring out when you're sick and when you're well, and when you need help. You're not sure which friends to make and whose example to follow. So in that first year, if you're a resident student, you live in a residence hall, with the support of a resident advisor (RA). You go to a common dining hall, and your teachers know you need support. There's a kind of safety net.

In your sophomore year, there's a little bit more freedom and responsibility. Maybe you live with five other students in a suite of rooms. You all share a bathroom, and you've got to clean it, and you as a group have to figure out how that's going to happen. You become more accountable and more self-managing. There's still an RA handy, but less direct supervision.

By the time you're a senior, you might live near campus in a shared house, where everybody has to make the residence run smoothly. You have a stake in running that household, and you have to work out problems to everyone's satisfaction and/or deal with the consequences.

This simple progression of residence life parallels the cognitive development that's taking place inside the classroom. In your first years, you acquire the tools of advanced learning, building on your natural gifts and the skills you learned in high school. You learn to manage your time, to balance knowing your limitations and pushing yourself beyond your comfort zone. Progressively, you make choices that affect the rest of your college years and life after graduation. You discover your most passionate interests. You learn what you do well. Perhaps more important, your growing self-knowledge includes confronting misconceptions about yourself. Maybe you don't really want to be a doctor, or maybe you discover you're not a homebody after all but want to travel and work overseas.

In the classroom, really difficult entry-level courses like organic chemistry and computer science weed out students who think they might like to be doctors or engineers, but don't have the right skills or talents for those careers. Likewise, the residential and social tests of campus life enable students to assess their social temperaments. For example, are you naturally more dominant or conciliatory? Do you incline toward leading a group of peers, or does your temperament thrive on solitary work? What communication style works best for you in a multicultural environment? Is your speaking style open and direct or more suggestive? Can you listen? Do your opinions matter to others, and why or why not? Can you persuade people to understand a well-considered decision?

From ages eighteen to twenty-four, people undergo significant developmental change along these lines and more. From responding to authority to working with peers, interactions in college preview the social dynamics of life after graduation. That could mean working in a global corporation or as an entrepreneur or as a Peace Corps volunteer in a faraway village.

The residential experience supplements classroom learning with a whole host of cocurricular experiences as well. I know first-year students who live in a Bentley dormitory in the Women's Leadership Community, participating in a program that creates leadership and community service opportunities. The RA advises and directs those eighteen-year-old women toward specific programs throughout the year, and to relationships with faculty who share an interest in women's leadership. These young women grow in confidence as they learn to read a room, articulate their ideas, negotiate plans, and become accountable for results. As they mature through four years, they test themselves in a relatively safe environment against their growing vision of how they will lead.

Mara Yule, a student from San Diego, points out that diversity still matters in a single-gender setting like the Women's Leadership Community. "It was an amazing experience for me to meet women from different backgrounds and interests, to learn about their lives and aspirations." In residence, students and their advisors break down the subtle and obvious

> In residence, students and their advisors break down the subtle and obvious stereotypes still prevalent in business because they see and feel the counterexample: women with business knowledge imagining, questioning, and often actually creating new businesses together.

stereotypes still prevalent in business because they see and feel the counterexample: women with business knowledge imagining, questioning, and often actually creating new businesses together.

"We have to make sure that the education isn't stopping at the classroom door," says Andrew Shepardson. "We as educators have to ensure those great conversations continue after seventy-five minutes in a philosophy class or a cross-cultural communications class or an organizational behavior class. They should weave their way into your conversation among friends over dinner. They should be part of how you manage your student organization. They should help you understand why your relationship with another person is not working, and how to fix it, or how do you exit the relationship? That's how people get significantly more from 122 credit hours on a campus than they will from the proverbial online degree earned in their parents' basement."

Shepardson puts the value of the on-campus experience in historical perspective: "A hundred years ago, people didn't think much about what we call self-actualization. But over time we learned there are things you can do to help young people become stronger, smarter, better able to grow into their full potential. This is a luxury, and the residential college environment should be about students becoming stronger, better able to engage the world around them, to step away from themselves and to think about who they are and what they want to accomplish as opposed to just going out in the world."

Students tell me that living away from home at college gives them an opportunity to break away from the strictures of family life. That's a healthy step for them into both decision making and accountability. (Yes, I do get emails from helicopter parents from time to time, demanding that their child be reinstated to the varsity sports team, or asking me to intervene with the professor who gave Johnny or Janey their first-ever low grade. I tell them as politely as possible that not everyone gets a trophy every time he or she does something in college. That's part of the experience as well.)

Every passage to maturity enables a student to gain two insights: how they succeed and how they fail. I mean more than just what actions lead to success or failure—I also mean the mental and emotional ways in which they react to success or failure. Can a student dust herself off and start again after failure, with confidence that she will eventually succeed? Can a student grow in confidence and in generosity, finding ways to share his success with peers or community? Leaders in business and elsewhere develop self-knowledge from success and failure that enables them to take risks and also to expand on their successes. The campus experience develops the same in students, especially the high achievers, away from those helicopter parents.

What Are Professors For?

President James Garfield, who graduated Williams College in 1856, once said of Williams president Mark Hopkins that "the ideal college is Mark Hopkins on one end of a log and a student on the other." Garfield's remark has long been quoted as testimony to the irreplaceable value of a strong relationship between student and professor. A century and a half later, the Internet provides a superabundance of information, but wisdom and intellectual growth still depend on the relationships of teachers and students. Those relationships develop most fruitfully in face-to-face encounters with professors inside and outside the classroom.

> The Internet provides a superabundance of information, but wisdom and intellectual growth still depend on the relationships of teachers and students.

On campus, life-changing relationships form between students and professors, and this is the mentoring that Gallup-Purdue found to be essential for success after college. Mentoring is more than support or interest, as Will Markow of Burning Glass Technologies details when describing his relationship with Dave Szymanski, an associate professor of natural and applied sciences at Bentley:

> I took multiple classes with Dave Szymanski, and if there was one lesson he impressed upon all his students, regardless of the course, it was that none of our actions exist in a bubble; rather, we are part of an interconnected social, economic, and natural system where our actions have far-reaching consequences across a multitude of stakeholders. And I think that, consciously or not, Dave's pedagogical approach embodies this systems-based philosophy perfectly.
>
> Just as Dave taught me that the consequences of my actions cut across a broader social, economic, and natural

ecosystem, his mentorship cut across my intellectual, inter-personal, and professional development. When I was in his classes, he pushed me to continuously improve my academic performance and unlock intellectual abilities and interests I never knew I possessed, even if my A was already in the bag. When I was applying for jobs, he reviewed my résumé, wrote letters of recommendation, and once even submitted an ap-plication for me when my computer broke fifteen minutes before the application deadline. When I was going through difficult personal times, including the deaths of multiple loved ones, he offered words of comfort and support. Even now, as I'm preparing to have my first child, he is still offer-ing advice from his own lessons learned as a parent. Suffice to say, he's been far more than an academic mentor; he's been a life mentor.

On a campus, students can find many such relationships, adds Markow. "Whether it was competing in moot court com-petitions with a team led by Franklyn Salimbene, pestering Dhaval Dave to teach me econometrics outside of normal office hours, working as a writing tutor under the direction of Greg Farber, discussing ethical dilemmas with Bob Frederick, or screaming about the nature of free will in the middle of class with Jennifer Cook for forty-five minutes, my experiences with professors gave me a new confidence in my academic abilities and cultivated a love of learning that I carry with me to this day."

The business leaders I know will tell you that email, vide-oconferencing, distance learning, and other forms of Internet communication haven't replaced all the benefits of face-to-face interaction any more than the telephone replaced the meeting generations ago. If they did, tech companies wouldn't spend fortunes for office space in Silicon Valley. The benefits of face-to-face interactions inspire the current vogue for open office design. There is something about interacting with people in the same room, over time, that creates and sustains relationships. The webs of trust and mutual benefit we call networking are commonly built face-to-face.

The same benefits bloom between students and their professors, coaches, and other college staff on a campus. Students acquire mentors who take an interest in them as individuals, and sponsors who advocate on their behalf.

Every successful graduate will tell stories of someone who took an interest in her and who gave her more than information. Studies by researchers at Gallup-Purdue find that these relationships are among the most significant factors resulting in a sense of well-being in work and life after graduation. Half the factors found by the report involved a mentor relationship with a professor.[2]

Bentley management major Shanell Mosley says a nonbusiness professor set her life on a new course. English and media studies professor Wiley Davi "not only challenged me to think in different ways but also pushed me to create awareness around issues of diversity and inequality. Davi also helped me learn that, although I was attending a business-focused university, there were so many things that I could do after graduation, including work in the nonprofit world." Mosley paired her management major with a liberal studies major in global perspectives and a minor in Spanish, and worked at the Multicultural Center in her spare time. She went on to work at AmeriCorps for two years and earned a master's degree in nonprofit management at Northeastern University. Today, she manages sports partnerships for the US Fund for UNICEF.[3]

Professors are also role models in obvious and subtle ways. Students observe how professors wear their authority on campus. Do tenured faculty treat students, lecturers, and staff with respect? What is their communication style? How do professors relate to their peers on campus and in the larger communities of their field of study?

Finally, there is the influence of a professor's enthusiasm. That might mean enthusiasm for the subject itself—the elegance of mathematics or the narrative of marketing. It might mean enthusiasm for the power of applied learning to change the world, such as when a professor of science contributes to solving environmental problems. It might even be love of learning for its own sake, beyond its "practical" value. I see this often in the liberal arts subjects that balance the practical study in a business degree.

At Drexel University, Dr. Cyndi Rickards is senior assistant dean for community engagement. Her keen interest in the problems of America's prison population changed the outlooks of many students. One of these was Larissa Bundziak, whose study at Drexel's Pennoni Honors College was focused on public relations. Bundziak tells the story:

> My summer going into senior year, I read the autobiography of a prison inmate. It really affected me, and so that year I took an elective offered by Dr. Cyndi Rickards called "Inside Out." We traveled to a local correctional facility each week and met with inmates about our age.
>
> Getting to know the inmates on such a personal, profound level changed my life. I had never really thought about the incarcerated population, and none of us were criminal justice majors, but [Rickards] pushed us to go out there and interact with people who we otherwise would never have met. We met in a room called a library—a room with a poster encouraging reading, and a few chairs, but no books. And I saw an opportunity. With Cyndi I constructed

a program called Prison Reading Project. Inmates and students correspond with each other about literature. Students provide inmates with literature. Cyndi helped me construct the program and then she helped me every other day to pitch facilities, providing me with her contacts to get this program going. It's now running at federal institutions in two states.

Larissa Bundziak was deeply moved by Professor Rickards's passion. "She is so dedicated to helping others and being a voice for the incarcerated, and teaching others what the incarcerated go through. She taught me to keep an open mind and extend my impact beyond people 'just like me.' She taught me to experience life differently."

The Role of the Community

When high school students visit Bentley, I urge them to pay close attention to the students they meet on campus. After all, they will spend much more time with their fellow students than with professors.

Christopher Joyce, who works in my office as a special advisor, learned this as an undergraduate at Bates College. He remembers that campus life "was a twenty-four-hour-a-day, hands-on, brain-on experience. I'd dive into a subject in a class and then sit next to somebody in the library who was working on a completely different area of study . . . My roommate was a math major, and we took no classes in common until junior year, when we said, 'All right, I'll try one of your classes; you try one of mine.' We were able to test and challenge each other's ideas and conclusions, approaching problems from completely different perspectives, and it made for a holistic, twenty-four-hour education."

Peer influences and relationships can forever change the way students approach their lives. Captain Timmy Donahue (Bentley 2006–2007), now a judge advocate in the US Army, applauded the hiring of William Kavanaugh as the head coach of Bentley football because he had known Kavanaugh as a peer. "I played with Billy. He was my captain when I was a freshman, and going in, I had teammates from high school who were older than me, who when they went to college, it was a very bad experience just going to the team and not fitting in with their teammates. That never happened to us, and Billy would never let that happen; he was welcoming of everyone."

Captain Donahue usually likes to work alone, but in his profession, that's not possible. His peer experience as a student helped him bypass his natural inclination. He says,

> In the Army, we do everything as a team. When we try cases, we always have somebody with us. When I was a defense attorney, there'd be two attorneys assigned to a case, and there would be eight attorneys in my district, and we would all bounce ideas off each other. And as much as I hated it at Bentley, there was a group project in every single class we had. It drove me crazy . . . but it helped me understand that you can't do it all by yourself. Today I think about all those times I had to work with people I didn't know, trying to figure out how we would complete our General Business 301 project.

That kind of stretching helped prepare him for his career as a military attorney.

The campus is a laboratory where students share different perspectives and life experiences among one another in a safe, relatively contained environment. The maturation process unfolds more successfully if you are engaging students in difficult conversations such as the ones we had among students, faculty, and staff around race relations following multiple protests of police shootings in places like Ferguson, Missouri; Baltimore; and New York City in 2014–2015. Students of all races came away with unexpected insights into one another's lives, and those many points of view helped them grow into wiser, more empathetic as well as more knowledgeable persons. Today we continue those campus conversations through a program called Bentley Brave.

On a campus, you can design some of that beneficial, dynamic tension into the system. One of the two staff members in our student affairs office in charge of dealing with Title IX and campus sexual assault awareness is a man, and he's talking to the football team and the hockey team as a peer. An African American woman is on the same staff, supervising fraternities. This kind of diversity can inspire unexpected and enriching conversations among peers. Bentley has a global-living dorm so that students can immerse themselves in the cross-cultural challenges and rewards of living with peers from other countries.

> On-campus experiences with peers help students strengthen traits needed in the innovation economy. If you can relate to a roommate who is very different from you, then you can develop the kind of empathy needed to understand a diverse population of coworkers or customers.

customers. When you work with teams of three, five, or a hundred persons of many different cultures and temperaments, you develop an understanding of team dynamics, and practice different communication skills. You learn to form a plan of action and persuade the team to follow it, and you learn to let go of your plan in favor of a superior one. You develop greater awareness of yourself as a leader, a follower, and a contributor. All these skills improve performance in the global business environment, and they are learned by experience and practice, not by reading about them online.

Students who commute, work online, or attend college part-time can and do develop these skills over time, but the learning opportunity is not as deeply baked into the environment. Necessity teaches them to manage their time and energy and attention well. Unfortunately, this approach leaves less opportunity to try out new experiences in a safe environment than that afforded students who live on campus.

Lately, the word *safe* as it relates to campus has been the subject of tense debate. I'm not talking about avoiding open discussion of uncomfortable topics. A college or university has to ensure the physical safety of students, but our job as educators is to stretch and challenge and support young minds, all at the same time. Here, I'm referring specifically to the understanding that taking an intellectual risk is key to mastering the study of business (or any other course of study). A safe learning environment means that students are not expected to answer every question correctly or limit their learning to rote memorization. They are encouraged to try novel ideas and innovative problem solving, even if the result would typically be called a failure in the marketplace. They know that they can speak up, ask questions, and propose answers that will be subject to critical analysis with a focus on the ideas, not the value of the person proposing them. The consequences of failure in such an environment are typically less dire than in work life (nobody gets fired; nobody gets injured), but the psychological and intellectual rewards of success are great.

Many of the world's most respected companies encourage employees to take risks by removing the stigma of failure when it proves valuable in the long run. Karen Kaplan, chairman and CEO of Hill Holliday, describes it as a departure from the win-lose thinking of business long ago. "You either win or you learn," she says, and both are valuable. Great leaders understand that they encourage learning when they promote the multiple rewards of taking risks. They know that their business will reward success, and they don't encourage failure for its own sake. Rather, they drive fear out of the workplace culture so that people can experiment.

But the majority of working people don't benefit from such advanced and nuanced management styles. Let's face it: in the average corporation, "failing while daring greatly" is not highly encouraged. That's part of the reason those workplaces are average. Everyone's trying to hit the deadline, make the number, satisfy the client, or check off the to-do list.

High-performing students sometimes have to be taught that playing it safe will deny them one of the great advantages of campus life—the chance to embrace the unfamiliar and, if they fail, to start over.

Students on campus are encouraged to form partnerships with people they don't know, and to learn, imperfectly at first, how to cooperate and build and grow and succeed together. In fact, high-performing students sometimes have to be taught that playing it safe will deny them one of the great advantages of campus life—the chance to embrace the unfamiliar and, if they fail, to start over.

Andrew Shepardson comments that campus life can promote a moral and emotional education in addition to the classroom curriculum because it gives students a safe place to test the values they've received as children. "Cognitive development doesn't occur when you talk to people and engage with people who think like you do," he says. "The opportunity for students to go away and perhaps throw away their parents' values can be painful for parents, but often students return to those values in a strengthened form by the end of college. You become who you are because you have the opportunity to step away and explore different ideas. It's certainly an American ideal: you are part of a democracy, and you are going to interact with a very pluralistic society."

Some of our international students experience this most intensely. Usama Salim is from Kuwait. He expected to study medicine in America, but began by attending Bentley as an undergraduate studying business, saying, "I get to experience a whole new growing-up phase where I live on my own. I'm paying the bills, living with roommates, and not having family help out as much as they do back home. I'm not just trying to get a job at the end of the day. I'm also buying experience here."

The Cocurricular Life

Ask graduates what their most memorable part of campus life has been, and they might well answer that it was extracurricular activities. As noted in chapter 4, at Bentley we call them cocurricular activities because we firmly believe in bringing classroom learning to nonacademic pursuits. We also strive to integrate what's learned outside the classroom back into the academic work. A business education should include all those skills I described earlier—the right-brain creativity as well as the left-brain technical skills. Some of those right-brain skills are best learned outside the classroom; they are critical complements to the left-brain "hard" skills.

For example, leadership is a skill you can study, and good leadership classes take students through case studies, showing the actions and analysis of both excellent and mediocre leaders. In cocurricular pursuits, students can apply the lessons they've learned to real situations. They compete and cooperate and bump up against the many subtle problems of leadership that call for the whole range of technical skills plus emotional intelligence, persuasion, and communication. If a cocurricular activity is really working well, a student might, for instance, perform a sophisticated financial analysis of an initiative, persuade others to join her in action, and then gather data over time to see how the "market" responds.

A prime example of this collaboration between the classroom and cocurricular activity is the Choose One Less program, which our students started in 2011 to reduce risky drinking on campus. The students started by studying the "prevention paradox," the observation that prevention messages fall flat among moderate drinkers, even though these drinkers account for 60 percent of those who experience negative consequences of drinking. Choose One Less was originally a collaboration among prevention professionals, health care workers, students, and faculty, and it used a multidisciplinary approach. For example, messages of the program were crowdsourced as students shared individual "One Less" decisions ("one less embarrassing story," "one less day of procrastinating," "one less night out"). Attention-grabbing data were popularized. ("By drinking six beers one night a week, a student consumes nearly 47,000 calories a year—comparable to 22 large cheese pizzas.")

"The message was a realistic approach," said Sophia Sirage, a 2015 graduate. "Instead of asking you to stop drinking altogether, it challenges you to turn it down a notch." Students were responsible for social marketing and branding the program, and they worked with Bentley administrators on data gathering, tracking, and analysis, and on academic syllabi. They also managed the program, and after one year achieved significant reductions in binge drinking on campus. Choose One Less was the Grand Gold recipient for the NASPA[4] Excellence Awards in 2014.

Bentley's associate vice president of university career services, Susan Brennan, believes that employers appreciate the skills that students develop by participating in cocurricular endeavors. She says, "Taking part in sports, student government, Greek life, and volunteer work show that you know how to work as part of a team, multitask, and deal with a range of perspectives, all of which are important skills to showcase. In addition, studying abroad shows that a student is able to take on new challenges, problem-solve, and adapt in unfamiliar situations. Being part of a student newspaper shows that a student is capable of critical thinking and meeting deadlines."

Employers also pay attention to students' job experience while in school. All types of jobs—whether on-campus or off—reveal a student's ability to manage multiple tasks and deadlines. A job as an RA or admissions tour guide is a prestigious position on campus. These jobs demonstrate that a student is trustworthy and dependable and can manage a variety of personalities. A job off campus demonstrates ambition and self-motivation as well as practical skills like time management.

Angela Su 2017, describes how the two kinds of learning and practice complement her education. "All my cocurricular activities I can see relating back to the business world," says Su. "I'm the president of the Bentley Asian Students Association, and that relates back to my management class. We're learning in class how to be a leader in a group, how to control a group, how to get things done as a group. We learn the characteristics of leaders and how different personalities can all work together. And so, in my management class I always think back to me being president of this group."

Bobby Mercer 2015, an information design and corporate communication major, is one of those students who throws himself into multiple cocurricular activities.

> They were really beneficial in the sense that we had a bunch of smart people with fresh information, getting to use what they just learned. I was a resident advisor on campus, and there were a lot of interactions with other students, and a lot of public speaking. These were different forums in which students could practice skills they would need in the "real world." I would talk to a room of two hundred kids during residential meetings. And that practice made me so much more comfortable during an internship, when I had to give a presentation to a room of two hundred coworkers.

Employers understand this and use cocurricular activities to learn the difference among candidates, adds Mercer. "When I interviewed for my postgraduation job, all the employers wanted to talk about were the cocurriculars. They'd seen ten other marketing students come in that day, and they all had the same degree. They focused on my experience as a resident advisor. It wound up that both of the people who were interviewing me had once been RAs when they were at college, so it was this whole bonding thing. Same with other clubs I've been a part of. They said, 'Oh yeah, I started a similar club . . . tell me about your experience with that.' It's a huge differentiation between you and your competition for that position."

Career Services

For decades, college career counselors joked that they were incredibly busy, but only in the last few months before graduation, as if students realized only at the last moment that they might need to acquire an actual job related to their major and also acquire career management skills before entering the marketplace. According to a new Gallup-Purdue Index report on career services, only about half of college graduates visited career services, and equal numbers reported that it was "very helpful" and "not at all helpful" (16 percent for each). A plurality of survey respondents found their college career services a tepid "somewhat helpful." On a more positive note, Gallup-Purdue found that when graduates have a positive experience with career services, they are almost six times more likely to say that their university prepared them well for life outside college and three times more likely to say that their education was worth the cost. And if these weren't reasons enough to bolster career services, the researchers at Gallup-Purdue found that those alumni reporting that career services were very helpful were more than two-and-a-half times as likely to donate to their alma maters.[5]

In recent years, leading colleges and universities have initiated more robust services, making career education a centerpiece of the college experience. Career centers are getting more funding, and, crucially, career educators are coming to the realization that anyone working in today's economy needs to acquire a set of career skills distinct from the typical course of study, yet also connected to classroom learning and service-learning. Susan Brennan sits on a curriculum policy committee alongside faculty to explore how classroom learning and new majors can tie in to job trends and market demands. Students graduating today are likely to have a dozen or more jobs over the course of their careers. They will have to move nimbly in response to the disruptions of technology, globalization, and the national and world economies. They will have to recognize new opportunity or, as in my case, be open to unexpected new opportunities. Moreover, people are coming to understand that working in a job unsuited to their skills, interests, and ethical standards is a ticket to unhappiness, whatever its pay or prestige. They have to develop greater self-awareness of how their temperaments, values, and skills translate into satisfying and successful careers. It's the job of career services to play the role of relationship builder and translator to make all these threads come together, and teach that perspective to students.

The great opportunity for students in a campus-based education is to learn and apply career management skills from the first day they arrive on campus.

Navigating the waters of a forty-year career is infinitely more complicated than it was one or two generations ago. The great opportunity for students in a campus-based education is to learn and apply career management skills from the first day they arrive on campus.

At Davidson College in North Carolina, students do just that. Jeanne-Marie Ryan, executive director of Davidson's Center for Career Management, describes a developmental model that students follow through their campus stay:

> From the first week of the first year, they are engaged with [us]. They do a Meyers-Briggs assessment to figure out who they are, what drives them, and where they want to go. The sophomore year is an exploration year, when they move from early investigation and assessment to answering in-depth questions about their goals, alongside and in conjunction with identifying and declaring a major. They engage with the Davidson Career Advisory Network, an online platform where they can engage with alumni who are professional leaders, in addition to parents and friends of Davidson who can help. This is also when we start robust job shadowing programs.
>
> The third year, we focus on clarification. Juniors spend time in campus seminars and workshops with employers and graduate schools and others. We have opportunities every day through fall and spring for such things as lunch-and-learn or even informal interviews. We have career treks to work sites so students can experience what it's like to work at, say, a company like Ingersoll-Rand. We host everyone from government agencies, managers in STEM fields, business innovators, and people from companies with strong entrepreneurial networks. And of course, in junior year, we expect all students to have an immersive professional experience—so, an internship or research experience or an externship.
>
> The senior year features what we call "transition to impact." It's launch year, and the president and I host a kickoff in the first week focused on making a transition to impact—that is, planning the steps you'll take to embark

on a life of leadership and service. By that time, a third of Davidson seniors already have identified their career and attained postgraduation positions. Others will continue to network and interview. For all of them, senior year career work focuses on day-one professional readiness, so that when they arrive in the workplace or graduate school, they are ready to hit the ground running and thrive with skills like salary negotiation, how to handle ambiguity in a large-scale corporate environment, and, most important, how to remain relevant wherever you are.

Bentley's Career Services Model

Susan Brennan points out that great career management skills, like cocurricular skills, both feed the classroom experience and are enriched by it. Her career services group designed a four-year process that shares the same goals as Davidson's while reaching deeply into the classroom. Brennan explains:

We are very deliberate about the timing over four years. In the first semester that students arrive, they are acclimating to being a college student, and they have a number of resources and programs to support that transition—joining organizations, living with roommates, being away from home, etc. So we say, "Don't worry about career search your first semester. Instead, attend our required course in your second semester that lays the foundation for career exploration. The whole course is just about exploration: who are you, what are your interests and aptitudes and strengths, and where do you want to go. You will think about defining your career parameters."

Soon after students arrive on campus, they complete a detailed assessment instrument called the Gallup Strengths-Finder. StrengthsFinder helps students identify their natural talents and most effective ways of working and learning. It relates these traits to possible paths of study and career, building on the observation that success is likely when people focus most of their effort on developing strengths rather than on fixing shortcomings. Once strengths are identified, they are incorporated into the curriculum. The proven model is progressively being woven into the student's experience of community and curriculum as well as in career work. Staff from both career services and student affairs have become StrengthsFinder-certified coaches through Gallup, and a group of trained students called Strengths Fellows act as one-on-one coaches for peers.

Brennan continues:

We understand that students are actually looking for a practical application, so we also teach an interactive, team-oriented class with a toolkit to find that first internship, and to succeed in it. At the same time, we know your twenties are the defining decade for learning, so we have two goals. One is really helping students to build identity capital, and the other is helping to strengthen weak ties and build networks. So that's the framework that we're now using around our career programming. It's not just about finding an internship; it's about finding yourself. Some of this is curriculum, some of it happens face-to-face, and lots of the work is done through CareerEdge, an online clearinghouse for all our services, events, opportunities, and learning.

In the sophomore year, which we call Experiment, students work with career advisors in partnership with general management faculty and student affairs staff. Alyssa Hammond, our director of career education and innovation, sees to it that every sophomore is assigned to a Career Colleague. Career Colleagues are upperclassmen who have gone through rigorous training similar to a service-learning model—they work side by side with career services. Each Career Colleague has a hundred or so sophomores assigned to him or her, and every day they have drop-ins when sophomores can come in to talk. This is a year when students practice career fundamentals.

For example, one important career skill is storytelling—about being able to tell your story and then gather stories from others. That's the new way of looking at a job interview. Integrating what they learn in the classroom and cocurricular activities, students learn to see their strengths in many dimensions. Developing their story also helps students develop self-awareness, which in turn helps them as they consider their majors. Students research specific organizations and talk to professionals in the careers that are relevant to those majors.

Between sophomore and junior years, students begin internships, many of them in nonprofit organizations. About this time, they also explore Career Communities, which bring students together with faculty, alumni, parents, and friends into learning groups that provide information, mentorship, and connection. Some communities gather around specific professions like accounting, human resources, or supply chain or operations management. Some focus on career choices like entrepreneurship or nonprofit management. And some focus on broad career categories like technology and consulting.

We call the junior year program Experience because students get into building career competency. This is the year that Len Morrison, our director of undergraduate career services, tells students to really take advantage of the many organizations we have on campus, because that gets the imagination going. Len points out that failure of imagination leads students to believe one functional role or industry is preferred over another. Exposure to new experiences and different people helps break down those preconceptions.

Like students at Davidson and colleges around the country, junior year at Bentley is a big time for internships. Through internships, students apply classroom and cocurricular learnings to real workplaces. As they deepen study in their majors, they find internships in fields that might be right for their early career path.

Brennan concludes, "We call the senior year Excel, when the career development course focuses on landing a job (for those who haven't) and transitioning to the workplace. Job search methods are continuously evolving, from informational interviewing to becoming skilled at online professional communities like LinkedIn. Learning to interview well is a big effort for many students, and they gain confidence as they learn how to prepare and how to practice. In addition to meeting potential employers, seniors continue to develop career skills online and in the classroom."

Students learn to thrive on campus and after graduation by experimenting in all these different on-campus settings—in the classroom, among peers, in the career center, or in formal and informal activities. Just as left-brain and right-brain domains work together in today's business environment, once-isolated pursuits like internships, sports, service-learning work, and even those 2 A.M. dorm-room debates come together in a campus setting to provide a rich and integrated experience. That is practice for life as well as career.

6

HYBRID LEARNING

Here's a scene witnessed in a class co-taught by Perry Lowe, a professor at Bentley, and entrepreneur-in-residence Woody Benson. The students' assignment: Create a marketing plan for a new high-tech consumer device. The client is real—a small start-up company. The need is urgent, with products shipping soon. Lowe and Benson fire questions at the students almost faster than they can answer.

LOWE	We have a one-time purchase, right? So, how much would you pay to acquire a customer? Would you pay $100 to get a one-time $400 customer?
STUDENT A	No, but I'd pay $50.
BENSON	Why?
STUDENT A	Because net revenue on the product is $100. That only leaves you with $50.
LOWE	That's better than where you were before.
STUDENT B	Yeah, but will that $50 cover your costs?
BENSON	What's wrong with this? Can someone give me a counterargument here?
LOWE	Okay, what's the first thing Woody said tonight? Sales, sales, sales, sales, sales. Start-up companies. Forget the breakeven.

> Forget everything other than the hockey stick. Everybody know what the hockey stick means? Hockey stick? What's the hockey stick? Help?

STUDENT C   It's exponential growth in units moved.

BENSON   If Uber started out worrying about breakeven, they never would have given away anything for free. The P&L is important, but at this stage, the revenue line is the most important. Figuring out what it costs to get customers by channel is the paramount. What gets you to the hockey stick? I don't care if you make a profit until that adoption happens. If adoption is exponential, I'd pay all day long! The pertinent question at this stage is not how much you're willing to make per unit; it's how much you're willing to lose per unit to get that critical growth in revenue. When that happens, profit's easy enough to make happen!

Benson and Lowe have a dynamic, no-holds-barred style in their teaching, and their corporate immersion class puts students in the arena of corporate decision making with real products, real corporations, and real deadlines—in this case, the start-up company asked this class for a pricing strategy. This is more than studying or copying a business case; it's learning by doing. Woody is not playing the part of an entrepreneur; he *is* an entrepreneur, bringing the benefit of his experience to students who in another setting would be his employees.

As we saw in chapter 3, employers today need graduates who possess skills typically associated with both liberal arts and business study. The modern workplace demands that hard and soft skills work together. Today, educators need to prepare students with a boundary-crossing blend of educational domains reflecting this evolution.

It is no longer solely what students learn in the classroom that carries them through their careers. An extended classroom that includes real-world experience is what truly prepares them to succeed. In their courses, students should have opportunities to interact with corporate partners, learn technologies that will give them an edge in specific industries, and work on group projects that hone collaboration and communication skills. All of these experiences prepare students to succeed in the working world.

Woody and Perry's students are engaged in a classroom experience we call "corporate immersion," a three-credit course that offers them an opportunity similar to a high-quality internship. Students in these courses work on solving current business problems for real companies. Executives attend every class meeting in person or virtually by teleconference, present their problem and relevant data, and let the students work on solutions in the classroom and between classes. Students are organized in competitive work groups of four to six. They are assigned deliverables and present them to company management. Each group can see the other team presentations—a rich experience in itself, as a class of twenty students might develop four or five different strategies to address the issue. The company's reaction to each proposal is shared as well.

Corporate immersion uses the hybrid learning model in a realistic staging of the corporate experience. Groups that have done data analysis have to get up and present their findings to corporate executives and classmates. Answering tough questions from Lowe and Benson, students learn to defend their ideas and see the flaws in their own arguments. They can fail and then rethink solutions. One of the most valuable lessons they learn is leadership. Although building leadership skills was not part of the program's initial design, the pressure of presenting solutions to real corporate clients revealed which students embraced the challenges of leading their peers.

Corporations participate in these classes because they're interested in improving business education, and for several good business reasons as well. They get the benefit of student and faculty perspectives and solutions unaffected by short-term thinking or company habits; they get an advance look at the best and brightest students and a head start on recruiting those star performers for internships and postgraduation jobs; and their managers sharpen their own skills as they present situations to students and critique their solutions. Companies who participate establish relationships with exceptional students they might otherwise miss. Smaller companies, start-ups, and long-distance participants in the corporate immersion program can compete for talent against larger, local businesses who rely on traditional internships.

For the corporate immersion experience to work, says Perry Lowe, three factors have to be in place: (1) the projects have to be chosen to match the skills of students—so that students can offer real, actionable solutions; (2) the right individuals from management have to be chosen and have to be committed to seeing the class through to its end; (3) faculty must manage expectations on both sides, and hold both to high standards, because that level of commitment mirrors the real corporate experience. At its best, corporate immersion isn't just like the real thing—it *is* the real thing. That is why it fits well into the larger context of hybrid learning.

Why Hybrid Learning Is Needed Now

In chapter 1, I listed ten features of hybrid learning. In this chapter, I'll examine a variety of ways that hybrid learning is practiced in colleges and universities today. What's exciting about these practices is that they are breaking from traditional learning models based on what the business, nonprofit, and public sectors say they need in graduates. As in any good experiment, the outcomes of hybrid learning practices are subject to rigorous scrutiny. In other words, educators are designing and evolving their models based on how well they work in the real world.

Career-minded business students and their professors typically emphasize one set of easily quantifiable skills (e.g., proficiency in accounting procedures) at the expense of an equally important set of hard-to-quantify skills (e.g., being able to communicate the meaning of accounting data in a clear way).

This reinforces the disconnect at the core of most educational programs that prepare graduates for careers. They risk ignoring important life lessons that cultivate soft skills that are needed for career success as well as personal fulfillment.

Bentley's dean of business and acting co-provost Roy (Chip) Wiggins points out that the stakes get higher over time. He observes, "In a few years, today's graduates will be considered for managerial, supervisory-level positions. That's when the softer skills become more important in their portfolio. In addition to getting that broad-based education, hybrid learning means students graduate with a sense of what they're going to do, and not just from a career perspective but with a sense of at least having been introduced to and starting to think about what their role in society is going to be."

A new model integrating hard and soft skills should be implemented at all kinds of schools—business and liberal arts, private and public, undergraduate and graduate programs. An integrated model would be especially valuable to community colleges, which award a lot of vocation-specific associate's degrees. Today's hybrid jobs, from nursing to accounting, require competencies outside of traditional domains.

Colleges have been under fire for as long as there have been colleges. (Bentley's dean of arts and sciences, Dan Everett, goes even further back, pointing to doubts about the humanities voiced twenty-five hundred years ago by Aristophanes in his play *The Clouds*.) Recent decades have seen a lot of debate about the cost of college, especially the return on students' investment in higher education. During the Great Recession and slow recovery that followed, media attention focused on the question of whether the cost of college was still justified in terms of its advantage in the job market. Stories proliferated about graduates unable to land their first job. Some educators turned defensive in their response, repeating well-known arguments supporting liberal arts education.

As those old debates are rehashed, the bunker mentality in some quarters obscures a more constructive conversation taking place among educators, education reformers, business interests, and other stakeholders. It is based on data showing that sitting at the feet of scholars is a pretty old-fashioned way to learn, and if that's all you do in school, you're not going to be prepared to take your place as an employee or a citizen.

> Sitting at the feet of scholars is a pretty old-fashioned way to learn, and if that's all you do in school, you're not going to be prepared to take your place as an employee or a citizen.

Reformers at institutions of every size, from the University of Michigan to your local community college, now see education as more interactive, experiential, and connected to the outside world from the first day of freshman year. We have learned that philosophy, ethics, English, and world literature are not incidental to career success in the twenty-first century but central to it. But that doesn't mean a well-prepared generation should shift from its emphasis on learning hard skills. Integrating the domains of knowledge—not artificially separating them—is the more effective preparation for career and life.

To reiterate my educational guideline, hybrid learning stands for *and*—not *or*. Hard skills *and* soft skills. Left-brain *and* right-brain. Self-reliance *and* interdependence.

This guideline was endorsed by a multiyear research project of the Carnegie Foundation for the Advancement of Teaching. It was called the Business, Entrepreneurship, and Liberal Learning (BELL) project, and it included close examination of ten colleges and universities, including Bentley. The study's findings are powerfully presented in Carnegie's 2011 book, *Rethinking Undergraduate Business Education: Liberal Learning for the Profession*.[1] It's required reading for anyone who wants to advance business education (and, for that matter, liberal arts education). The authors wrote of "reciprocal integration" in which "each of these domains [liberal arts and business or practical learning] must serve as both crucible and catalyst to animate the educational potential of the other."[2]

Educators can disagree on which subjects should appear on either side of the *and*'s I mentioned, but institutions that best prepare graduates overall are combining and integrating those hard and soft skills. For the record, I believe that 90 percent of Bentley's faculty, having experimented with this model for a number of years, would agree. Their belief shows in the enthusiastic recalibration of courses in business and liberal arts.

Foundations of Hybrid Learning

Hybrid learning combines the best of professional education (in Bentley's case, business education) and the liberal arts. It develops critical thinking, professional skills, cultural literacy, and domain-specific knowledge in a single course of study.

Hybrid learning combines the best of professional education . . . and the liberal arts. It develops critical thinking, professional skills, cultural literacy, and domain-specific knowledge in a single course of study.

The power of combining these domains is evident in people who, whether because of temperament, determination, or genius, have done so without the benefit of a structured program. Think of medical writers like Lewis Thomas (*The Lives of a Cell*) or Atul Gawande (*Being Mortal*), whose right-brain gifts communicated detailed left-brain information to a popular audience. Think of Neil deGrasse Tyson and, before him, Carl Sagan, astronomers who brilliantly communicated advanced scientific concepts on television. Think of American polymaths like Paul Robeson, Margaret Fuller, and Benjamin Franklin, all celebrated for accomplishments that combined left-brain and right-brain talents. And think about the professor of mathematics who can communicate the relevance and beauty of advanced calculations, or the software engineer focused on experience, who designs beautiful, delightful interactive apps using advanced computer coding.

Bentley's Dan Everett describes hybrid learning this way:

If you can master the complicated thinking and mathematics of accountancy you might be a good accountant. But accountancy alone will not prepare you to think across the range of contexts that the successful citizen will need to navigate. Likewise, if you learn to find, interpret and build ideas about the past on primary sources and become a superb historian, what is it you know about the business behind the stock news that signals boon or bane to your career prospects? The way forward is to help students to master both liberal arts and professional ways of thinking and foundations of knowledge. The idea that you cannot do both is based on a false dichotomy . . . namely, that professional education and liberal arts education represent a disjunction rather than, as we believe, an optimal conjunction.[3]

What is an optimal conjunction? That depends on the institution, its faculty, mission, and special domains. A hybrid learning model for medical school, for example, would have a blend of left-brain and right-brain disciplines different from that of a business school. But both models would emphasize technical mastery and intellectual flexibility; both would combine hard skills like assessing data with soft skills like empathetic communication.

The optimal conjunction for a business school can be found at the intersection of a particular business discipline, a student's aptitudes and goals, and the market demand for her skills. For example, a student might combine a major in economics and finance with a liberal studies major in earth environment and global sustainability. If he did, he would be well suited to develop a business plan for a growing solar power company. Or she might select a public policy major and match it with a broad-based business studies major—and then help change the way US presidential campaigns manage campaign finance. Or someone might put together a left-brain interest in accounting and a right-brain interest in ethics and corporate responsibility; Wall Street is in need of investors and business leaders like that. These are real examples I've witnessed in recent Bentley graduates.

Hybrid learning can be implemented at the undergraduate and graduate levels, in any academic domain. Catherine Usoff, dean of the Graduate School of Management at Clark University, has said that teaching methods once confined to liberal arts studies should be used even in the study of rule-bound fields like accountancy. She writes, "By explicitly reinforcing the communication, multiple perspectives, and thinking skills in the accounting courses, students are made to demonstrate the necessary integration and will be better prepared for the workplace."[4]

A discipline like history develops in business students a respect for diverse experience and a sensitivity to culture that benefits anyone working in a globalized organization.

In a similar vein, Bentley associate professor of history Christopher Beneke argues that a discipline like history develops in business students a respect for diverse experience and a sensitivity to culture that benefits anyone working in a globalized organization.[5]

Hybrid learning at colleges and universities goes by different names and is practiced in different styles. For example, Brandeis University has a liberal arts focus, and most of its business majors are double majors. (Its undergraduate business program became one of its most popular majors just three years after its inception.[6]) At West Virginia University, the College of Business and

Economics and the School of Public Health created a dual-degree program that weaves business skills into the study of public health.[7] And at Georgetown's McDonough School of Business, students in a freshman seminar called Ethics of Entrepreneurship take on a semester-long project designed to help them sharpen their critical thinking and writing skills in a global and social framework, grappling with ethical questions entrepreneurs typically encounter as they start a business.[8] Robert Morris University in Pittsburgh uses a model it calls engaged learning, and students have to participate in at least two of six learning areas to graduate.[9] Antioch University, with five campuses nationwide and programs that span the globe, is focused on adult education and has a long history of high-quality experiential and competency-based education. Explains chancellor Felice Nudelman, "Competency-based education has to be responsive to what's going on in [any] industry, so it really begs a different type of curriculum, much more integrated, interdisciplinary, and focused on workforce needs. Competency-based education provides a comprehensive approach to education and helps students demonstrate that they have mastered the skills that are transferable to work life."

In short, different forms of hybrid learning are emerging in every corner of business education. Jeanne-Marie Ryan of Davidson College's career center observes that because the future will bring more and more hybrid jobs, those institutions who want to stay relevant will move to hybrid learning of one form or another.

One Goal, Different Models

I'm lucky to know a number of education leaders who have been modeling hybrid learning for some time. To contrast different models, here are programs at four colleges where hybrid learning is showing excellent results, as described by those institutions' leaders.

Paul LeBlanc—Southern New Hampshire University

"I have a theory that higher education is called upon to do one primary job in a given time period," says Paul J. LeBlanc, president of Southern New Hampshire University (SNHU). "And the one we're being asked to do now is better alignment with workforce needs."

LeBlanc's influence on higher education spans multiple domains, including pioneering work in educational technology. In 1997, he created the first degree program in e-commerce. After arriving at SNHU in 2003, he turned a small online education program into a national powerhouse. Of special interest is his work in competency-based education. It speaks to the need for hybrid learning to break out of rigid curriculum guidelines and focus on the day-to-day requirements of today's jobs.

LeBlanc explains the latter:

> Competency-based education (or CBE) is establishing a lingua franca, a common language, between the supply-side institutions of higher education and the demand-side institutions of employers. Traditionally, higher education talks about courses and credit hours and transcripts. If I'm an employer and I see that you got a B in general psychology, I can infer some things. But I don't really know what you know, and I certainly didn't know what you could do with that knowledge. I routinely will say to a roomful of CEOs or HR directors, "Now, raise your hand if you've hired somebody from a reputable four-year college or university who doesn't write very well," and every single hand in the room

goes up . . . In the competency-based programs, we're finally talking about what students can do with what they know. And employers talk about what employees must do.

> I can imagine a more flexible kind of curriculum design for some institutions based on real-time employment data. Changing job requirements can be understood early by analyzing massive job databases.

With the common language of competencies, educators can certify that their psychology majors and business majors can also write well, and that's incredibly valuable to employers. Going deeper, I can imagine a more flexible kind of curriculum design for some institutions based on real-time employment data. Changing job requirements can be understood early by analyzing massive job databases like those at Indeed.com or Monster.com. That analysis can be applied to curriculum or even individual courses of study. When a graduate is certified as competent in a certain skill, his or her value to employers increases.

LeBlanc suggests two examples of current jobs that would benefit from competency certification: "If you're a journalist today and you went to J-school, you're a very good writer. But guess what? You're also going to be expected to take digital photos and send those in; newspapers are not going to afford a separate photographer. You'll also have to be able to jump into Photoshop and clean up the raw image before you send it to an editor who's halfway across the world. And, by the way, you'd better understand how to blog—and, by the way, use Twitter; and, by the way, depending on where you are, you may need to have encryption technology on your phone, and more and more and more. So, all of those worlds start to blend.

"If you are a patient-facing person in the health care system, it's almost guaranteed you are now interacting with technology a lot more than your predecessors did five years ago. If you're leading a distributed software engineering team, you'd better be culturally aware. You can say 'this line of code sucks' to your American team and be fine, but say that to your Indian team and it would be shaming and disrespectful."

What if a skill (especially a technical skill) becomes obsolete? Does that mean customized credentialing is bound to fail? LeBlanc answers,

> As we increasingly approach a time when lifespan at nineteen will be a hundred years, the notion that only 4 percent of your life would be spent in higher education is antiquated. What we're going to see is more disassembling of that four-year continuum. There's still a real hunger among eighteen-year-olds to go live on a campus and have that quintessential college experience, no doubt. But for a lot of people it's going to be an associate's degree for now, and then what I call "stackable credentials" over the years as jobs career paths require. Maybe ten years after college, the world has changed enough to require a different set of credentials. Look for the emergence of nanocredentials or microcredentials in the coming years.

The challenge, he adds, is to establish a common set of standards across the universe of certificate programs appearing today. But that challenge has been met in the past in such professions as health care, and if higher education and employers can invent those common standards, competency-based higher education will prepare many for careers in the innovation economy.

Rick Miller—Olin College of Engineering

Rick Miller, president of Olin College of Engineering, is focused like a laser beam on educating innovators. His approach to hybrid learning reflects the practicality of an engineering perspective.

A lot of folks think that innovation means taking an idea from a science experiment, throwing it over the wall to the tech transfer office, finding a jar of pixie dust that you sprinkle over it, and magically turning that into a business. We think that innovation always happens at the intersection of three independent spheres:

One of them is feasibility because nothing happens that's not feasible. That's what traditional engineering schools do. Then, an idea also has to be financially viable as a business. That's what business schools do. The third sphere is whether an idea is desirable. Lots of solutions are both feasible and viable, but they don't sell because not enough people want them. A really successful innovation is one that changes the world so profoundly that people can't remember the way it was before it came in, and that only happens if people change their behavior in ways they had not imagined. So you have to understand people in order to create innovation. That's the domain of the liberal arts.

Miller continues with a powerful example, saying, "Some of the most important innovations of the last decade did not come out of a new kind of physics or a new kind of Nobel Prize. Take, for instance, Facebook. What does it sell? It sells an opportunity to tell your story to people that you care about. That matters because every human being has a fundamental need to be the most important person in somebody else's life."

To create innovators at an engineering school, Miller and his colleagues reached beyond the boundaries of their campus. He says, "We want innovation engineers who are equally versed in feasibility, viability, and desirability. We did this by creating a program among three colleges: Olin College of Engineering, where the feasibility is taught; Babson College, where the viability is taught; and Wellesley College, where the desirability is taught. We put a team of teachers in the same room, and student's can't tell you [which sphere] they're learning, because we mix them all together."

The result is both immediate reward and a big ambition, he concludes. "Olin students are in enormous demand, and we've been visited by 350 universities in the last few years, studying our model. We hope to change the way engineering is taught in America and throughout the world."

David Angel—Clark University

"Liberal arts education can't stand still, and we can't defend the status quo," says David Angel, president of Clark University, a private four-year liberal arts school. He continues,

> We have to ensure that a liberal arts education serves the students as they graduate into the world we have today. I think we're going to find that every college and university in America is going to move towards blurring the lines between the learning that takes place in the classroom and learning that takes place in the world . . .
>
> Decades ago, you could graduate from college knowing a lot of stuff but not quite knowing how to translate that in creating value in an organization. We wanted to change that,

so we began by asking a lot of employers around the country about what kinds of skills and capabilities they were looking for in graduates, and also what kind of skills and capabilities marked folks who were really flourishing in their organizations. Of course they want problem-solving skills, and we also heard a lot about resilience—people who hit a bump along the way but don't get knocked off track. Employers want people who can come up with creative, third-way solutions.

So we set ourselves up intentionally by asking, "If you really want to set people up to have those skills, how would you do it?" You can't do it in the classroom. You have to place your students out into the world, facing authentic challenges and problem-solving skills in real situations. If you bring that together with the classroom, you have some magical results.[10]

Angel focused on a particular problem faced by colleges changing their model: "The challenge that a lot of colleges and universities have when you think about building these skills is how you go to scale," he says. "It's easy to do this for 10, 20, 50 students, particularly the smart, charismatic ones . . . but how do you make sure that all students have these opportunities? The solution we came up with is to tap our thirty-five thousand alumni. We seek them out to agree to host a student on a project anytime, anywhere around the world."

Clark University's overall program design is called LEEP— Liberal Education and Effective Practice. LEEP components are similar to Bentley's hybrid model, integrating classroom teaching, guidance and mentoring, workplace experiences, and cocurricular activities. In particular, the "effective practice" component emphasizes students' creativity and imagination, resilience and persistence, and the ability to collaborate with others. As a liberal arts school, Clark stresses continuous engagement with the "big questions" of human cultures and societies, as well as the natural world. And as the university joins those who support lifelong learning, it also promotes an ethos of a lifelong habit of "critical self-reflection" in its students.

Angel says, "The key challenge is to work well with all constituencies (alumni, business partners, parents, and friends) and in particular the faculty. They initially will not be comfortable with this increased emphasis on learning opportunities [outside the classroom]. In our experience, faculty become comfortable because the strongest advocates for educational integration in this country are the students themselves. When faculty see the results of LEEP on the students, they get very excited about the new vision of integration."

Bruce Leslie—the Alamo Colleges

Bruce H. Leslie is chancellor of the Alamo Colleges, a group of five community colleges that together compose one of the largest postsecondary educational institutions in Texas.

"We developed a set of three policies that we call the Alamo Way, which includes a framework we call principle-centered leadership. We have a theme we call 'A Leader in Every Chair.' The idea is that for today's organizations to be flexible and highly responsive to change, everybody's got to lead."

At the Alamo Colleges, Leslie says, a highly specific set of skills was most appropriate.

We decided after much engagement with our employer and political communities that the concept of soft skills was too amorphous. We refer to them as the "essential skills" [needed] to be effective employees or effective leaders. We decided to go with the leadership skills model, and partnered with Franklin Covey Company around the 7 Habits of Highly Effective People [first described by Stephen Covey in his best-selling book by that name]. The employers in our community know that program and teach it to their own employees. They said, "Yes, we know that program, we teach it to our own employees. If you could certify your students have those skills when they graduate, we will put them in the front of the line for employment."

Beyond preparation for employment, says Leslie, the program helps students be more successful *in* college.

Our partnership with Franklin Covey is a very strong relationship, and we have a license authority for pretty much all of their product, including certifying our own teams to teach the 7 Habits. So these are increasingly important strategies to help students be successful in college, finish college, which has been a big national issue with hundreds of thousands of students across the country that have some college but no degrees or certificates. With our program and an internal development program from Franklin Covey called the 4 Disciplines of Execution,[11] we have increased our degrees awarded by 110 percent in just the last few years. Our rate of increase is two-and-a-half times that of any of our other Texas peer institutions.

The unusual model is making an impact beyond improved completion rates, says Leslie. "Recently, a doubtful trustee asked Alamo's student trustee, 'Sami, I understand that you started taking the 7 Habits course. What do you think about it?' Sami is about thirty-five. She has a family, she manages a store at the mall, and she said, 'You know, I consider myself a leader.

So far I've only been through habits one through three, but [the training] has already told me that I have so much more potential than I ever realized.' After that, the trustee became a supporter."

Other elements of hybrid learning at the Alamo Colleges are similar to those at other institutions, such as experiential learning, internships, and service-learning. One exciting addition to Leslie's portfolio of services is a model for teaching financial literacy to students, many of whom have never learned the basics of managing personal finances. As of 2016, students were being hired on each campus to be public advocates for financial literacy to their peers.

Leslie concludes by describing the size of his task in southern Texas: "The five Alamo Colleges serve sixty thousand students each year, and so we're moving to roll that out to all sixty thousand so every one of them will have the opportunity to get the certification and hopefully change their world."

Bentley's Model of Hybrid Learning

Bentley's undergraduate liberal studies major is an example of how hybrid learning works. Its creator, former dean of arts and sciences Kate Davy, was a phenomenal creative thinker. Working with others, she conceived a way to apply the liberal arts to a business major.

After completing core business courses, business majors add a fully integrated liberal arts major to their business curriculum. For example, a marketing major might add a major such as global perspectives. Working with faculty advisers, she creates a custom set of higher-level courses that integrate these disciplines. Then she completes a long-term project in both majors, documenting how the skills and information from each discipline work together. Documenting this integration is key to raising the student's awareness of the importance of both domains as well as spurring innovative ways to coordinate them.

Kate Davy's goal was for students to use both majors actively in assignments, not just see the connections between them. A typical challenge: come up with a marketing plan to bring a successful US-based product line to a global marketplace. Rather than just run a set of numbers and marketing scenarios, a student has to integrate work from his global perspectives class—analyzing cultures, economies, spending patterns, and even political factors and incorporating that information into his marketing plan.

The hybrid learning concept was so successful for Bentley's business majors that we eventually applied the program in reverse to create a liberal studies major. It is an optional double major in which students combine a business discipline with a major in a liberal arts subject. For example, an undergraduate major in sustainability science can add a broad-based business studies major that's thematically related—say, operations fundamentals or finance. That student is thus equipped to model real-world sustainability projects in terms of their operational or financial feasibility. In a construction project, that could lead to innovative thinking on how energy conservation, green energy, and cogeneration can work for an office building. It would bring up questions about public policy, supply and pricing, permitting, state politics, and the ten-year direction of public utilities in a particular location.

This is how smart decisions are made in private industry and in nonprofit organizations. Hybrid learning encourages twenty-year-old undergraduates to wrestle with such trade-offs and innovations in a supportive learning environment.

Another form of hybrid learning recently introduced at Bentley is a six-credit course co-taught by a business faculty member and an arts and sciences faculty member. They team up to teach the two thematically related subjects, one from business and one from arts and sciences. For example, a management professor joins a colleague in film studies to help students analyze interactions in film scenes, seeking deeper meanings in facial expressions, body language, and diction. This can help students understand their own person-to-person interactions, opening them to act in new ways in a business environment.[12]

One recent six-credit hybrid learning course was co-taught by professors Jeff Gulati (political science) and Bryan Snyder (economics). Called Faction and Fiction: The Politics of Economic Policymaking, the course explored the fractious interaction of economics and politics. Students compared data on the results of an economic policy (such as supply-side economics or the North American Free Trade Agreement) with the way that the policy was "sold" to the American public. During the semester, students practiced both quantitative reasoning (in economics and public polling) and qualitative persuasion (how a policy achieved political viability). This is how the real world of politics and policy works.

In a hybrid learning environment, students are constantly on the alert to make connections in fields that are typically separate. It's no coincidence that this results in a spirit of innovation, experimentation, and risk-taking.

Hybrid learning is deliberately flexible at Bentley, and exactly how the integration will occur is figured out between a student and her advisers. The goal is to inspire innovative combinations, to empower and encourage, and, yes, to require students to dive deeper and deeper into the unknown as they combine disciplines. In a hybrid learning environment, students are constantly on the alert to make connections in fields that are typically separate. It's no coincidence that this results in a spirit of innovation, experimentation, and risk-taking. We see students pursuing their most passionate interests while also learning the broader set of skills that hybrid learning delivers.

At the graduate school, Bentley's flagship MBA program uses the hybrid learning principles in a different form. The eleven-month program moves through four academic modules (we call them quadrants): innovation, value, environments, and leadership. Each theme weaves multiple hard and soft skills. For example, the innovation quadrant studies psychology and decision making, theories of creativity, business design (including how to assess alternative designs), and the relationship between business and strategy. The environments theme requires MBA students to merge understanding of social contexts (organizations, countries, and cultures), economics, and technology to manage the dynamic forces exerted on business inside and outside an organization.

Like the undergraduate hybrid learning program, the graduate model stresses extensive interactive with professors and peers, emphasizing synthesis and debate. National and international fieldwork is required, meaning that business skills have to operate in tandem with study of global cultures and international economies.

Nadia Stoyanova-Lyttle came to Bentley's first one-year MBA program from Bulgaria as one of twelve non-US students in a cohort of nineteen whose innovation module was taught by professors specializing in marketing, human design and user experience, psychology, and English studies. That combination mirrors the integrated approach required to develop products in today's innovation industries like computer services and health care devices. Here's how she describes the unorthodox experience:

> One of our tasks was to create a project that would challenge our own skills, perceptions, and stereotypes but also engage everyone in the group. I remember everybody bouncing ideas off each other, trying to determine what topics would relate to most people in the class. We used different means of expression—painting, video, even a stand-up comedy routine!
>
> I presented a topic completely unknown to the others: young women leaders from Bulgaria. The leaders on my list featured the gay and lesbian rights movement, a chairperson of UNESCO, and other political leaders, as well as Bulgarian business leaders. I played a video excerpt without translation and then gave my classmates a summary of the messages they had heard. And the key was presenting them in the leaders' own words, in their own language, so the class would have to understand the meaning of their speeches even though they weren't speaking the language.

The innovation module was serious business, Stoyanova-Lyttle recalls. "It was a constant competition, like most MBA programs are. And yet because of its diversity, intensity, and requirement for innovation, people were very dedicated to finding the best in themselves and revealing the best in their classmates."

One more quality distinguishes hybrid learning: it prepares students for work and life by pushing them out of their comfort zones. One feature of success in today's global innovation economy is the willingness to take risks of all kinds—financial, intellectual, and even emotional. I believe that college is exactly the time to confront your blind spots, to be challenged on all fronts, and to learn the extent to which you can become expert in the complicated dance of hard and soft skills that characterizes so many innovators.

Four Critical Venues for Hybrid Learning

I've stressed that hybrid learning entails an awareness of context in applying professional and liberal arts studies, and this is where it takes a long stride away from the classic, cloistered ivory tower. Hybrid learning pays close attention to such environmental factors as economic conditions, cultural values, questions of law and ethics, and the accelerating rate of change. These factors affect both the arts and sciences (try keeping up with the pace of scientific or historical discovery) as well as business.

In our experience at Bentley, we see four venues in which students benefit from a conscious application of hybrid learning practices: classroom, cohort, community, and corporation.

In the Classroom

Hybrid learning in the classroom requires students to be actively engaged in problem solving. They formulate and test hypotheses. They apply critical thinking to potential scenarios and develop multiple solutions to complex situations. Professors in the classroom spend little time lecturing and lots of time encouraging on-the-spot synthesis using tools at hand (from web research to Bloomberg terminals). Then, like Woody Benson and Perry Lowe, they challenge students' answers. This resembles certain phases of a postgraduate professional education—think of medical interns making rounds with a doctor, or moot court in law school. The difference is that it takes place very early in a student's career and is fully supported outside the classroom by faculty, staff, and corporate partners (see the section "In the Corporation").

Technology is necessarily part of the hybrid learning classroom experience. For example, when a class is working on a marketing program, laptops and licensed databases can be used to conduct research on the fly.

Marketing professor Ian Cross points out that, a short time ago, his students could go on to marketing careers with technologists down the hall ready to process data for them. That's no longer true, and his other title, director of the Center for Marketing Technology, speaks to the new world of left-brain/right-brain integration in marketing. He describes the hybrid learning blend of domains in marketing:

> Certainly my students need a firm grounding in the liberal arts and a mastery of theory in subjects ranging from marketing research to psychology to consumer behavior, but they also need to be able to use the digital tools that transform theory into practice, even while those tools are transforming the marketing profession itself. Marketing students today need Google Analytics, search-engine marketing, and social media like Instagram, Google+, Facebook, Twitter, LinkedIn, Pinterest, and Periscope. Next year they'll need even more tools. They need to know how to analyze user experiences, develop websites, and create personas that will

define an inbound marketing campaign using the HubSpot platform. They need to know what content marketing is, how to create a content calendar, operate a customer relationship management system, establish metrics that define success, and execute strategies that achieve marketing goals, based on data-driven objectives and tactics.[13]

So much for an employee relying on colleagues down the hall to do all the technical work. In hybrid learning, technology is more than an end in itself, and even the technologists benefit from hybrid learning studies.

Computer science major Angela Su relates hybrid learning to the postgraduation working world. She says, "If I were going into a company working for the IT department, I would know how the other departments all relate to it because I have a grounding in business studies. Someone coming from a more technical orientation with just a computer science background would know how to do all this technical stuff, but she wouldn't be able to see the bigger picture."

A few years ago, senior lecturer Mark Frydenberg of the Computer Information Systems (CIS) Department redesigned Bentley's computer lab to immerse students in an environment similar to a modern software development "sandbox"—that is, a place to experiment on software outside of critical systems. The CIS Sandbox operates on a bring-your-own-device basis— students show up with laptops, tablets, cell phones, and so on—and instead of isolating themselves in front of terminals, they collaborate openly on projects and innovations, challenging and teaching each other. Two unexpected benefits of the CIS Sandbox emerged in the first year: visiting companies used the space for presentations and workshops, and students themselves shaped and improved its day-to-day operations. Now the

CIS Sandbox is a busy learning space hosting its own events, workshops, and tech fairs as well as providing a venue to study and debate current issues like "fake news" and data security.[14]

The professor acts as a source of expertise, as in a traditional classroom. But the job requires much more than knowing more than the students about a particular topic, or criticizing and assessing their work. She and her colleagues must keep driving toward the integration of disciplines that is at the heart of hybrid learning. For example, when a student team reaches a solution to a financial problem set, the professor might challenge members to defend the solution to a skeptical "client," modeled by other students. Or she might encourage a discussion of the ethical implications of an investment, asking students to consider social justice, sustainability, or other issues that otherwise wouldn't be part of the conversation.

Formalizing the interdependence of hard and soft skills, day after day in practice, enables what takes place during the precious classroom hours to become a habit. And habit is powerful.

Great professors teach students to make such connections in the classroom because they know the interconnections that exist in real-world situations. And universities treasure those great professors. But making those connections shouldn't depend on the values of one inspired teacher. It should be required as part of the classroom experience because understanding and harnessing those interconnections make graduates better at everything they do. For the most part, this is the way the world works; it certainly is the way business works. Formalizing the interdependence of hard and soft skills, day after day in practice, enables what takes place during the precious classroom hours to become a habit. And habit is powerful.

The magic of applying hands-on practice in the classroom is made more powerful by professors dedicated to real-world learning and candid, ego-free discussion. Here's one memorable example.

Professor Tim Anderson, who led the Sociology Department at Bentley, permitted me to attend his Native American Studies class from time to time. He lives part of the year in Montana and holds honorary membership in the Crow Nation. In his class, he used a traditional Crow talking stick to support unfettered debate. The talking stick was passed around, and the person holding it had to speak with absolute courage and candor. Nobody could interrupt the speaker. The talking stick is a sacred object; in Anderson's class, you didn't abuse the privilege of taking your turn with the talking stick or disregard anything someone else said. Anderson's talking stick exercise subverted the typical power structure of a college class and forced people to broaden their outlook. (Yes, he made me take a turn with the stick, and I was nervous!)

Anderson is a classic example on a business school campus of someone who breaks through the power façade of a classroom (which mirrors the power façade of a boardroom) and forces discussion of the consequences of business decisions, both the good and bad. I think he walks on water, and many of his students over many decades would agree.

In the Cohort

Hybrid learning outside the classroom is typically a team effort, with members of the student cohort dividing up complex projects and working toward solutions in study groups. This is common in graduate programs because there's so much work to do in a short time. What distinguishes the hybrid team is the breadth of strengths used to tackle the projects. Analyzing a real-time case (as in the corporate immersion class with Benson and Lowe) requires separate looks at operations, finance, marketing, manufacturing, technology, and more. This mirrors strategic business situations that also require a wide range of analysis.

Jose Gutierrez graduated from Bentley in 2014 with a bachelor of science in finance. He's now a technology associate at Morgan Stanley in New York City. He says his experience with teams both inside and outside the classroom made a huge difference in his education.

> Whether you consider yourself a leader, a follower, a motivator, or a role player, you can learn a lot about yourself when you are part of a team. Before I started college, my group work experience was limited to my high school's Jeopardy! team in Honduras, where I grew up. We won five hard-fought national championships. Little did I know how well that experience would serve me in college.
>
> As part of a team working on an antibullying program through the campus Service-Learning and Civic Engagement Center, I found myself working with a large group of passionate people with very different personalities. I learned early on that you can't always pick who you work with. Just like in the workplace, there were both pros (developing

collaboration and leadership skills) and cons (dealing with difficult personalities and people not pulling their own weight) of working in a group.

I found that both hard and soft skills were critical to success. I obtained hard technical skills through classroom work and internships, but the critical soft skills came from working in the antibullying team. I became aware of my greatest strengths and weaknesses through collaboration with my peers. For example, I learned I was much better at engaging crowds in school rallies than planning the logistics of those events. I developed a loose, easygoing leadership style in response to group tensions. I learned to recognize others' work styles and manage to their temperaments. I paid more attention to competing solutions from others; I sharpened my critical thinking skills.

To other students I'd say, next time you're assigned a group project, don't groan. Go into it with an open mind. Take the challenge. You'll be surprised by what you can learn about yourself.

Working on cross-disciplinary teams, students also practice project management, leadership, and managing group dynamics (including personal traits like reliability). Students of typical college age are maturing intellectually and psychologically, and we can enable the maturation process by designing programs that emphasize the skills they'll need later in work and life. We know that empathy, communication, respect, risk-taking, and open-mindedness flourish in such an environment. Students can even learn to manage failure together if they perceive failure as a safe part of the learning process. Not incidentally, executives tell me they want students who have learned to turn failure to their advantage, as it's so likely to happen over the course of a career.

Bobby Mercer 2015 also believes in the importance of teamwork across a cohort. He says,

> When you step out of the classroom, the ideas are still flow-ing so that we actually apply what we learn to other activities. For example, I was involved in the Wellness Educators on campus, and we had events throughout the semester. Using my communications major, I was able to develop marketing plans and see them through to fruition. Some school proj-ects go until the due date and then they're over, but this was an ongoing effort. For wellness events, we designed visual media for the campus, delivered social media, and created a subset of the wellness website. All of these were real-world applications of what we learned in marketing communica-tions classes. We applied them and measured the results and then brought that back to the classroom.

Working together across disciplines to synthesize a solu-tion breaks students out of their specialization. Bobby, who does digital marketing today, finds that his exposure to finance and accounting is invaluable, whether he's updating a company's investor page or reading a 10-K report. He can quickly surface the most relevant information for investors and present it in a way that someone who had only studied com-munications could not.

In the Community

Service-learning and the work that takes place off campus are integral parts of preparing for life after college. Service-learning is more than volunteering. It is an academic pedagogy adopted by many institutions and codified at Bentley by one if its earli-est proponents, Dr. Edward Zlotkowski, in the 1990s. In the simplest terms, it means "classroom to community to classroom." Students study a subject area inside the classroom and, upon reaching proficiency, go out into the community to take on service assignments that tap their new skills. They then return to class to share what they learned about applying those skills in the field.

Service-learning and the work that takes place off campus are integral parts of preparing for life after college. Service-learning is more than volunteering. It is an academic pedagogy adopted by many institutions.

Service-learning integrates class work with real-world practice in two designs. One is called "embedded," whereby every student in the class pursues a service component as part of course work. The other adds an academic credit to the traditional three-credit course at Bentley. Students earn the fourth credit by going into the community for two hours a week (twenty hours per semester). Their project must connect in some way with what they're learning in the classroom. For example, students in a psychology course might work in an afterschool program for children in low-income housing; a marketing course might develop a public relations strategy for a nonprofit; or business students might analyze organizational challenges for a social welfare agency. The students don't just parachute in to help, though. The requirement to report on and analyze their experience back in the classroom is key to the value of service-learning. Yes, it's a great thing to volunteer. But the hybrid learning philosophy suggests that integrating at least some volunteer work with class work is excellent preparation for postcollege life. The service work calls both for technical skills and for right-brain skills like empathy.

Jonathan White, director of the Bentley Service-Learning and Civic Engagement Center, built on Zlotkowski's ideas to the point that more than a thousand students and a hundred faculty participate in the program every year. He has seen that service-learning in the community magnifies the benefits of students' classroom and cohort experiences.

Speaking of the city where Bentley is located, White says,

Waltham is a diverse town in terms of race, ethnicity, nationality, and also social class. It's remarkably integrated. My wife and I live in Waltham. This is our home. We're dedicated to it because it's our community, and because its diversity offers rich opportunities for our students. When students go out to help in the community, they come back feeling like they can't possibly give enough because every time they go out to give, they come back having received more. They come back with their lives changed by the richness of what they learned, which we can't teach in the classroom. I can teach a class on diversity and open up a textbook and have students read about it, and they do learn. But when I send them out into a deeply diverse community where they serve and interact with people of different cultures and different thinking and different backgrounds, they learn ten times more than they would in a classroom alone. Connecting the classroom to the community is essential and impactful.

For some students, it's the global community that provides the most valuable hybrid learning experience. Canadian-born graduate Edith Joachimpillai works as a research analyst in the

Global Economy and Development Program at the Brookings Institution. She learned the hard skills of quantitative analysis in the classroom, but says her policy work is informed just as much by her field experience.

> A lot of the creativity in my work comes from my arts and sciences background, from math to Mandarin. I was a fellow at Bentley's Valente Center, where you study one topic from all angles, and in my year the topic was nature versus nurture: Are we born with minds like a blank slate, or are there innate capabilities and restraints to people? That study was completely on the arts and sciences side of the spectrum. I took professor Kristin Sorensen class on global commerce and human rights in Chile. We traveled to Chile for two weeks and studied the human rights violations and the dictatorship that happened during the seventies. I went to China as part of my Mandarin coursework. To have experienced a developing country as a student now informs my policy work in a way impossible for someone who only lived in the United States.
>
> The combination of business and arts and sciences has taught me to think of problems critically from at least two dimensions. In my work, the reasoning and quantitative analysis comes from the business side, but linking data to the historical and cultural context of global economies enables me to see things in ways I otherwise wouldn't.

Joachimpillai concludes that the combination also prepared her for the intense, boundary-crossing work at Brookings. "The work of a think tank is to delicately balance the line of journalism and academia. Work does not stop outside the office. My team is exceptionally brilliant, and the Global group [at Brookings] is multiethnic . . . which makes for the best potluck dinners!"

Academic competitions enable students to experience the pressures and rewards of solving real-world problems before a different community: the community of professionals outside of college whom they hope to join in their careers. One of the most difficult and prestigious of these is the Fed Challenge, a competition that casts students as economists for the Federal Open Market Committee. Advised by professor of economics David Gulley and associate professor of economics Aaron Jackson, students prepare intensely to recommend monetary policy actions to a judging panel of Fed economists.

Edith Joachimpillai represented Bentley at the Fed Challenge, and recalls, "We have time and time again competed with the likes of Harvard, MIT, Dartmouth, etc., in macroeconomic policy, which is not easy. And as somebody who now works in the same building as the chairman of the Federal Reserve, I don't think it's a small thing, either."

Erik Larsson 2015 also participated in the Fed Challenge, and it helped him land a job at the Federal Reserve after graduation. "When I was interviewing for this job, one of my interviewers told me he had also participated in the Fed Challenge. He said that working at the Fed is like doing the Fed Challenge in terms of conducting economic analysis and its implications for monetary policy, except that it's for real. Now I get to do it eight times a year (once for every Federal Open Market Committee meeting)."

Jonathan White notes the connection also between community work and real-world work skills by posing this scenario:

Imagine yourself as a corporate employer interviewing students who come from a variety of different universities, with a variety of different backgrounds. They're all telling you,

"I took advanced accounting, I got my 3.8 GPA, I was in the Honor Society, I did this and that." And then you've got this other group of students who add, "I managed forty students at a community partner site that brought education programs to low-income students. Here are all the problems I ran into, and here is how I solved them. Here's how I reported the results to faculty and service-learning staff. When I ran into a roadblock with my program, here's the solution I created, and here was the result . . ."

Given that kind of experience, I know who I would hire. One of the distinctions I love about Bentley's Service-Learning and Civic Engagement Center is that many programs recreated and run by the students themselves— including the internal program to keep track of all the service programs. Corporate recruiters like the fact that students exercise leadership within the professional functioning of the university. And corporations spot those candidates early if their acquaintance happens before graduation, in the corporation itself.

In the Corporation

Ninety percent of Bentley students complete at least one internship during the course of their education. Seventy percent complete at least two. Working for a company is a natural opportunity to practice the hard skills and soft skills they will need after graduation.

I'll add that the internship experience shouldn't be limited to companies. Rachel Spero spent her first undergraduate internship in government. She remembers that the hybrid learning program enabled her to jump in, prepared to understand the big picture.

Rachel recalls, "A couple years ago, I interned at the Ways and Means Committee in the Massachusetts House of Representatives. My internship merged public policy with finance and accounting. One of the people who I worked for told me that it is important to have an understanding of business with whatever you do, but for public policy of that kind—writing budgets and tax plans—business skills are essential. A lot of students who want to go into the political field don't understand that."

Internships are standard experience for college students these days; employers expect most students to have work experience before they graduate. Unfortunately, internship programs have a quality-control problem. Maybe a student will have an insightful learning experience as part of a decision-making team, or maybe the student will spend most of the internship isolated in a cube, updating a database.

In a high-quality internship, a student is doing more than making copies all day; he or she is also present to study how decisions are made and to implement significant action plans. The business partner in an internship program needs to give the intern the same accountability as a regular employee, and still review the intern's work and teach the intern the ways in which work gets done (what business consultants call "tacit knowledge"). Colleges can encourage quality by engaging corporate partners committed to providing a meaningful work experience to students. But quality control is still difficult, especially with strained corporate budgets and untrained or time-pressed managers.

Another problem is that most internships don't pay. Students who must support themselves by working twenty or thirty hours a week—some of our best students—don't have time for unpaid internships. Time also is a factor for athletes and others deeply involved in cocurricular activities. How can you take a full course load, fulfill your commitment to a team sport, and still have time for an internship?

The most enthusiastic corporate supporters of hybrid learning are managers in charge of finding talent. They are looking for people with crossover skills. Imagine their reaction to a résumé: "You matched sustainability science with a corporate finance major? Our energy division needs you now!"

Laboratories like the corporate immersion course are the ultimate examples of hybrid learning. They aren't imitating the world of work but participating in it. They demand that students make the connections between left-brain and right-brain domains long before graduation. The experience trains business students in capabilities they would not otherwise anticipate—capabilities we see in great managers and leaders everywhere from the heights of corporate life to the halls of government.

The relationships established during an internship can last long after graduation. Connecticut native Samantha Vlahos discovered this when, midway through her senior year, she traveled from the University of Alabama to New York City to find an internship. Says Vlahos:

> In January 2015, I interviewed with Lori Bizzoco, the founder of NV Media, Inc. and a website called Cupid-sPulse.com, a celebrity entertainment website. The minute I hung up the phone, I knew she was a woman I needed to know. It wasn't just her impressive background that won me over, but it was her passion for her craft, her business, and her ability to share her knowledge with those who were eager to learn. (I'm not kidding, the woman was teaching me things in the interview!)
>
> I was given opportunities typical interns may not have had. For example, in my first month, I launched an Instagram account for CupidsPulse.com, and was challenged to think strategically about how we would grow this account organically. After the first few months, our team was able to grow the following to over two thousand users. As time passed, I was pitching stories to the media and received placements in the *Atlanta Journal-Constitution,* FOX News, MSN.com, and more. Eventually, Lori grew so confident in my abilities that she had me managing a team of interns. During my senior year at the University of Alabama, I continued to work with Lori and grow professionally. She taught me how to network properly.
>
> In the spring of my senior year, we would talk once a week. She continued to help me network, and taught me how to craft a résumé and write an email that will

actually get read. She would challenge me, asking, "Who do you think you should be contacting? Why should I tell them about you? Why should I send them your résumé?" She was tough, very tough, and made me better professionally.

Their professional relationship continued long after Samantha moved on to another company, to manage public relations for two leading pharmaceutical firms. She says, "Lori is my work mom. I still talk to her several times a week, and talk to her about what's happening in my career like I talk to my real mom about what's happening in my life."

7

THE PROMISE OF A NEW GENERATION

All of the students and recent graduates whose stories I've told in this book belong to a unique social group— those whose college experience took place since the turn of the century. As I listen to them, work with them, and try with them to make change for the better, I believe they can give educators and the organizational world they are now entering great reason for optimism. They are the generations that will truly change the world.

I'm an unabashed fan of the Millennials, the generation born between 1981 and 1998.[1] They were the ones who inspired me to leave the practice of law to work in higher education. I'm doubly enthusiastic about their successors, generally called Generation Z, those born after 1998, who are now arriving on campus. This combined new generation of students—I'll call them collectively "today's students," even though many Millennials are now in the workforce—is distinctly different from the generations that preceded it. Just as the innovation economy called for a new model of preparation for work, the abilities and culture of today's students offer clues for how that new model can be most effective.

—❧——————

Just as the innovation economy called for a new model of preparation for work, the abilities and culture of today's students offer clues for how that new model can be most effective.

—❧——————

Every generation has common qualities because its members faced similar conditions growing up. While acknowledging that each student is an individual, and being careful not to let generalizations form all policy, we in higher education should consider these conditions closely. They suggest which teaching practices will work best now and in the future. Let's compare what we know about today's students, the Generation Xers who came before them, and the Baby Boomers who preceded Generation X.

My generation, the Baby Boomers, grew up at a generally prosperous time; the civil rights movement, the Vietnam War, and the sexual revolution were the background against which we formed our views. We were the first to grow up with television and a media landscape that glamorized individualism and rebellion.

Generation X, which followed, came of age amid accelerating boom and bust. These "latchkey kids" were the first modern generation to have two working parents. They entered the workforce in the 1980s and 1990s, when both economic opportunity and economic uncertainty were on the rise. They generally mistrust authority, but have joined the corporate world in droves, pushing change from within. They value independence, competence, and flexibility. They are the first truly tech-savvy generation—for example, making email the preferred communication medium at the office.[2]

This is not to suggest that Baby Boomers or Generation X have identical views within their respective cohorts, just that they share a deep level of common experience. The same is true of Millennials and Generation Z, which makes today's students an especially exciting generation for an educator. Let's consider why.

First, today's students matter based on the size of their cohort. In 2015, Millennials became the largest age group in America, numbering more than 75 million. The Boomer population peaked in 1999 at almost 79 million and is now declining. Generation X, born from 1965 to 1980, peaked at about 66 million and is also now declining. The Millennial population will peak in 2036 at about 81 million.[3] In the first quarter of 2015, they passed Generation Xers as a percentage of American workers. This means that the workforce—the managers and entrepreneurs and consumers who drive the economy—is increasingly part of the Millennial generation.

Generation Z is even larger. According to the US Census Bureau, it makes up about 25 percent of the US population today and will remain there, peaking at about 112 million in 2050.[4] They are entering college now, and significant numbers of Generation Z graduates will be part of the workforce soon.

The second obvious reason for these generations' importance is that they are soon to be the largest group of consumers. Companies that don't understand them are ignoring the greatest business opportunity of our time.

I've heard their corporate elders complain of a generation full of "trophy kids," who are "too entitled" and who lack a strong work ethic and require too much flexibility from employers. They say today's graduates should wait for their turn to lead, just as previous generations paid their dues. They say this new generation is addicted to their screens and doesn't maintain appropriate boundaries between work and private life.

This what's-the-matter-with-kids-today attitude ignores some key facts. Millennials as a group have career ambitions and expectations that are quite similar to those of Boomers and Generation X. All want recognition and advancement. All are skeptical of corporate claims of loyalty to employees, and all are open to "jumping ship" if a better offer appears. And Baby Boomers and Generation Xers are just as enthusiastic about new technology as their younger counterparts.[5]

> Who wouldn't want to take the most educated, skilled group ever delivered into the marketplace and use its talent and tastes to further their business, their mission, their values?

Like employers, educators should get past the myths and build a strong understanding of what makes these generations unique. They should ask, "How can we engage those qualities, behaviors, and beliefs to best prepare them for career and life after graduation?" If we get it right, the opportunity they represent to business, the economy, and civic life is enormous. Who wouldn't want to take the most educated, skilled group ever delivered into the marketplace and use its talent and tastes to further their business, their mission, their values?

Two Generations, Different from Their Predecessors

These generations really *are* different in terms of their relationship to education. Although each generation has some unique challenges and advantages, the confluence of changes in business, technology, economy, and culture has never worked quite so powerfully to shape a generation. Consider the interplay of the forces:

- Globalization and falling borders and barriers (e.g., international trade)
- The speed of change in business, including:
  - Greater deployment of nimble, flexible teams that form and break up as the need or opportunity arises
  - Changing job requirements, including skill sets, experience, and even temperament or emotional intelligence
  - Rapid product cycles
  - Regulation, capital flows, and policy
- Specific information technologies:
  - The ubiquity of information, in ever more customized forms
  - The continuing move from text to video and sound (voice) in applications, which is poised to sweep education, commerce, and other interactions[6]
  - The way big data challenges long-accepted "truths" with facts and analysis in fields from financial planning to journalism

- Mobility (e.g., handheld devices, 24/7 connectivity)
- Many-to-many communication (e.g., by encouraging online students to grade each other's papers)
- The burgeoning power of artificial intelligence to "imagine" and create innovative solutions in product design, manufacturing, and even service industries

Today's college students master arcane subjects with relentless hard work, yet also adopt complex technologies with ease. They challenge professors as no generation has before them, and also go the extra mile for those professors who challenge them.

Most students arrive at college as young adults, still forming the foundational attitudes, capabilities, skills, and habits that will serve them through a lifetime. This includes the capacity to recognize gaps in their knowledge (before they dive too deeply into specialization), and a pretty good capacity to change their minds as they absorb new knowledge. Their energy is high. They possess a powerful and at times paradoxical combination of self-absorption and selflessness. They might worry all day about their career choices and then work all night, unpaid, tutoring English as a second language (ESL) in a nearby town.

Students today surprise me with their attitude toward authority. They expect me to be a 24/7 president, available to them on a first-name basis as a mentor, advisor, and networking resource (just as business leaders are). And I encourage it by asking them to call me Gloria and not President Larson so that they feel comfortable talking to me on campus, coming to my campus home, and reaching out to me for help. Of course, if they ask me to fix a bad grade, a parking ticket, or a broken air conditioner in the dorm—which they often do—I send them straight to student affairs. Most important, they listen to me and challenge me, and maybe I'm still something of an outsider in higher education, but I confess I love that attitude.

One example is a recent graduate who approached me for a reference, but not because he didn't have a job lined up. He had already been accepted into a prestigious leadership program at a large national insurance company. He wanted the reference because he thought he really belonged in the nonprofit world, and he wanted my help should he decide to leave the insurance company. Both his mother and I had urged him to give the insurance opportunity a try, believing it was a good match for his Bentley education and personal skill set. Still, I listened to what he had to say about taking that same skill set and knowledge in a different direction, where he might better impact the lives of others, and I wrote the reference. As it turned out, he did leave the insurance company just short of a year after graduation and is now serving in a leadership position at the American Red Cross, making that larger difference in the world he was seeking. I'm glad he challenged me, and I'm glad I listened.

What the Research Reveals

These might be the most researched generations in history. Looking at the data, I see a complex and intriguing picture of today's students. Millennials and Generation Z are as a group more sophisticated, worldly, and prepared to lead than their predecessors. This is largely a result of technology and globalization. They grew up with the Internet and digital devices. They came of age as globalization boomed, giving them a wider outlook. As consumers, they had far more choices than preceding generations for everything from news media to music to groceries. As students, they learned from childhood to find information online. They are natural researchers, whether hunting for information for a college assignment or for a bargain on clothes.

They grew up in a more visibly diverse country in terms of racial and ethnic demographics. They experienced rising public acceptance of diversity, from the Americans with Disabilities Act to the legalization of same-sex marriage. This doesn't make them all doctrinaire liberals, but on issues of inclusion and diversity, their attitude is "What's the big deal?" Whatever their individual opinions, the social landscape of their formative years provided a more expansive view of our country and our world.

They are much more accustomed to seeing women and men as equal in the workplace, and have strong female role models in business, nonprofit, and political life and often at home. They have significantly more education than other generations, with women leading the way.[7]

The Millennial and Generation Z cohorts have not had it easy. The oldest of them were just starting their careers as the dot-com bubble burst and the attacks of 9/11 shook the nation's sense of security. The slow recovery, the financial crisis of 2008–2009, and the Great Recession that followed had significant impacts. Research shows that graduating into the workforce during a recession has long-term negative career and income effects.[8]

In addition, these students have learned hard lessons about money. Many watched their parents struggle financially through the last recession, and many have struggled personally with housing costs, credit card debt, and yes, student loans.[9] They keep more than half their savings in cash, whereas previous generations invested at a higher rate.[10] They are employed at a higher rate than those who have not attended college (as with the general population), but feel exposed when companies cut back on hiring, salaries, or benefits because they are the junior employees. Millennials change jobs an average of 6.3 times between the ages of eighteen and twenty-five, but this doesn't necessarily translate into higher wages. In fact, it takes a young adult about four more years to reach the middle of the wage spectrum than it did in 1980.[11]

> Today's students are practical and realistic. They began careers in a global marketplace, competing for opportunity with other American graduates and also with people their age around the world.

As a result, today's students are practical and realistic. They began careers in a global marketplace, competing for opportunity with other American graduates and also with people their age around the world. Many saw a negative impact of globalization and technology on their parents' jobs. They also saw the world's insatiable appetite for American culture. They've carried that global perspective into their working years.

They are pragmatic about education and career. In recent years, students choosing which college to attend have placed increasing importance on a college's rate of postcollege job placement.[12] They want to come out of college with marketable skills and, they assume, high levels of adaptability, in part because they know that today's jobs require them to be flexible, team directed, and interdependent.

They tend to be optimistic about the future. Almost half in a 2014 Pew Institute survey said that America's best years are still ahead. Millennials responding to the survey also were significantly more likely than other generations to say they either had enough money to lead the lives they want now or expected to in the future.[13]

A few other qualities of this generation stand out to me: Millennials do not want to just read textbooks or hear lectures, even on detailed subjects. They would rather learn by doing, preferably in groups or teams. They have been conditioned by all forms of technology to retrieve information in quick bites. Assistant professor Liz Brown teaches business law, taxation, and financial planning—all topics that require long concentration on detail. She says of today's students, "Their attention spans are short, and they seem to be getting shorter all the time. It's doubly challenging for me as a professor to make sure that I engage people for an hour and twenty minutes when traditionally *nothing* engages them for an hour and twenty minutes. In an hour and twenty minutes, they'd be looking at seventy-three different sources of information. I'd like them to focus on one!"

It's a common assumption that generations are broadly different because each reacts to its immediate predecessor by adopting a different set of priorities. Thus it's said that whereas Baby Boomers were largely driven by the social aspirations of the 1960s, Generation X was shaped by the economic and political disappointments of the 1970s. The latchkey kids of Generation X became the security-seeking, independent Yuppies of the 1980s. In turn, as Millennials who grew up in the go-go 1990s tend to be optimistic, technical, and confident, so we might assume that their successors in Generation Z, who were children during 9/11, Hurricane Katrina, the Iraq and Afghanistan wars, and the Great Recession, might grow to be risk-averse and perhaps more pessimistic than their parents or older siblings.

I don't believe that these two generations are diametrically opposed. Instead, I see a cultural continuum from the Millennials to Generation Z, and social research seems to bear this out. Millennials are comfortable with information technology, using two screens at once; Generation Z is embedded with information, using as many as five screens in a day (smartphone, TV, laptop, desktop, tablet).[14] The older generation easily embraces email and reading digital forms of traditional media, such as newspapers; the younger generation is more likely to communicate with images and to favor text messaging over talking on the phone. Generation Z is coming to college now in a time when the use of video and infographics to convey serious information is exploding, and that conditions how they learn. Learning to comprehend and create good infographics, for example, is somewhat like mastering cartography or even a foreign language. In this age group, girls are much heavier users than boys of mobile visual platforms like

Snapchat, Instagram, and Pinterest.[15] So perhaps some old truisms like "girls are more interested in communication" continue into the smartphone age.

Whereas all previous generations have been *consumers* of media and experiences, these generations are used to being *cocreators*; that is, they participate widely in the creation of media content (from commenting to reposting messages to creating videos). They are habituated to crowdsourced experiences, from the trending topics on their social media feeds to flash mobs.[16] Fully a third of them have already collaborated online with classmates in learning experiences.[17]

The experience, culture, and habits of these two generations support a move to hybrid education. Millennials and Generation Z will thrive in a college experience that takes advantage of their abilities.

How Educators Can Adapt to Today's Students

Millennials are bringing so much to the world, from technical acumen to social consciousness. If we give them an education that balances left-brain and right-brain domains, with a real-world orientation, they're going to hit the ground running in a very different and more impactful way than any prior generation. They will emerge as the leaders we need and the world citizens we admire.

Just like businesspeople, we in higher education must adjust our practices and methods to make the most of the opportunity these generations present. Colleges must not alter their "product" just to suit changing consumer tastes. We shouldn't dilute our expectations for quality, ethical behavior, and expertise to accommodate short-term trends. Yet for us to further the institutional mission, we must constantly deliver an education relevant to today's student and today's society, preparing young men and women in the best ways possible for work and life.

The hybrid education models described in chapter 6 are based on more than the needs of the workplace; they also respond to the distinctive qualities of the generations I've discussed. The next sections identify those qualities and how hybrid education suits Millennials and Generation Z.

Millennials and Generation Z Are Practical, Pragmatic, Hands-On Learners

Colleges that offer students a more hands-on education through experiential learning and service-learning help today's students transition to the workplace by replicating the workplace. Corporate immersion projects with bottom-line impact on real businesses outside the academy raise the stakes of success, while at the same time teach the day-to-day priorities of business. It's one thing to know that cash flow is important; it's another to adjust your proposals to fit into the cash-flow picture of a real business. The experience is invaluable.

> Corporate immersion projects with bottom-line impact on real businesses outside the academy raise the stakes of success, while at the same time teach the day-to-day priorities of business.

I envision tomorrow's business school as more learning laboratory than lecture hall. The hybrid learning model places great emphasis on experimentation, improvisation, and feedback, and rewards rather than disdains changing direction based on new information. Because today's students already have the intellectual and technological tools to conduct research, education must lean toward creating scenarios, implementing action, and seeing the result.

Earlier, I emphasized the importance of well-designed internships, and these also speak to the pragmatic streak in today's students. Their response to the economic challenges since 1999 is to emphasize the practical outcome of attending college, not just for career but also for their intentions to participate in society.

Recommendations: Preview the practical outcomes of classroom study. Devote more class time to project-based learning and "flip" the classroom by putting more passive learning (e.g., lectures) online. Devote more discussion time to scenario modeling and analyzing outcomes. Reward initiative and experimentation and encourage intellectual risk-taking.

Their Behavior and Expectations Are Profoundly Influenced by Digital Technologies

It's not just that these generations are adept at using technology; they are the first to grow up entirely immersed in the particular qualities of instant, pervasive, interactive information. Earlier generations adopted new digital technologies at about the same rate as Millennials, but they adopted them later in life, when much of their conscious and unconscious habits were well established. Millennials and Generation Z have interacted with screens from infancy. They switch more readily to new platforms of communication. For example, in 2012, researchers at the Pew Research Center for Internet, Science & Tech found that 90 percent of Millennials and Generation Z used social networking sites, compared to 65 percent of Baby Boomers. That's a big difference, but dig deeper and the data show an even greater contrast: whereas 67 percent of Millennials and 91 percent of today's teenagers use social networking on their mobile phones, only 18 percent of Boomers do. That's not because smartphones are cheaper than laptops; it's because Millennials have adapted their lives more fully to smartphones. They employ mobile big-data applications in shopping, travel, education, and more.[18]

Millennials' comfort with digital media in many forms makes them less dependent than previous generations on the classroom for some traditional college hallmarks like large introductory lecture courses. As noted in chapter 5, massive open online courses (MOOCs) take advantage of this. MOOCs have their own problems, including low completion rates, and they certainly haven't replaced the classroom. But there is a great sorting process under way between information that can be acquired anytime and anywhere versus skills that can only be learned through engagement with professors and peers. This platform-agnostic generation adopts the most convenient practices with ease. A college which claims that nothing will replace a particular learning activity had better be prepared to prove it.

In addition, these generations question the utility of some learning, because they're accustomed to information technology acting in parallel with everyday life. Earlier generations learned to use the technology called a slide rule, until calculators ended that. They checked spelling using dictionaries and memorized spelling lists until spell-checking software made those skills irrelevant to daily use. As instant translation software improves, Generation Z students might question the utility of language study. Hybrid learning will answer that question by pointing out that language is a key to understanding cultures, not just a practical tool for communication. In a similar vein, the study of art or music might have no immediate "practical" value to a business student, but it broadens the mind and trains a person to understand the dance of discipline and creativity. In today's classroom and workplace, that is necessary understanding.

Recommendations: Integrate online learning (including third-party MOOCs) and outside relationships, such as professional mentoring, with coursework. Develop collaboration activities that use social media. Create more multicollege partnerships online. Focus on the intellectual benefits of topics and courses of study that might be "practically" replaced by technologies. Teach students to recognize when information is relevant to a subject and when it is merely entertaining or distracting. Teach concentration and "flow"—that is, mental absorption in a topic or task.

They Are Skeptical, and for Good Reason

The often-repeated charge that Millennials are cynical is misplaced. Cynics believe that people and institutions are insincere and motivated by self-interest alone. Skeptics, in contrast, might have a much more positive or hopeful view . . . but they want evidence.

Millennials have earned their right to skepticism. Consider the example of the financial world, which bracketed Millennials' conscious memories with the savings and loan scandal of the late 1980s and the financial meltdown of 2008. Both events, which caused enormous economic damage, were characterized by corruption and deception on a vast scale. The intervening years brought wholesale layoffs and the "right-sizing" of workforces, while executive pay soared.

Public confidence in political and social institutions of all kinds has plummeted in the last twenty years. Here's a sobering data point: only 19 percent of Millennials agree with the statement "Generally speaking, most people can be trusted."[19]

In this skepticism lies a great opportunity for educators. It inclines Millennials toward evidence-based inquiry, which, among other things, is the foundation of the scientific method and the motivation to learn for oneself. Whether studying finance or sculpture, every student needs a healthy dose of skepticism.

By harnessing their skepticism and technical acumen, universities can equip Millennials and Generation Z with a particular focus of critical thinking. We must build a curriculum-wide set of tools to discriminate between reliable and unreliable sources of information. The Internet, and social media in particular, masks and magnifies falsehoods. Fake news sites distribute myths and propaganda, and they are effective because they look and sound just like the real thing (and conform to users' preconceived ideas). Without a critical eye on the source of information, students and graduates are natural targets for all kinds of manipulation.

Another way to harness skepticism without descending into cynicism is to encourage students to leave their echo chambers on social media. Let's revive the practice of requiring students to argue both sides of a case, citing confirmed facts and reasoned opinion. Social media is an especially rich place to do this, and also to train people to make critical arguments without shouting others down, making threats, or dismissing opposing views.

> Millennials do not hold higher education in such awe that they won't ask for proof that studying at our college will prepare them to succeed in their world.

Of course, the same skepticism will greet college administrators or professors who take a "trust me, I'm in charge" attitude. Millennials do not hold higher education in such awe that they won't ask for proof that studying at our college will prepare them to succeed in their world.

In addition, this generation is less impressed than previous ones by rules they consider arbitrary, but they are highly responsive to proven expertise, creativity, and accomplishment. They like to judge for themselves whether their professors and other educators are doing a good job, and whether the methods they teach are the best ways of solving a problem.

The institution itself should be a place to encourage students to step up. I work at a university filled with smart and creative young people. In fact, some of the best campus improvements have came from students and younger staff members. For instance, Amanda King, Bentley's director of sustainability, regularly enlists students to offer ideas around energy conservation, recycling, and other school sustainability goals. It's Millennials, with their integrated focus on people, planet, and profit, who can give Bentley and organizations of all types a fresh perspective when it comes to challenging economic, environmental, and social issues. They should never wait to be asked for their points of view!

Millennials care a lot about the results of their work, but are more inclined to experiment with different ways of reaching goals. They have little patience for bureaucracy. Members of older generations might feel the same, but Millennials are more likely to be open about their opposition to corporate red tape and work for work's sake.

Recommendations: Teach critical thinking by requiring students to research opposing answers to questions, relying on objective and verifiable facts. Encourage self-awareness by having students describe, defend, and also counterargue their preconceived ideas. Examine the notion of trust with such studies as negotiation strategy in business, politics, and interpersonal affairs. In all majors, include study of the capabilities, as well as the use *and* potential abuse, of data analytics.

They Are Open to New Experiences, Trusting the Wisdom of Crowds More Than the Claims of Untested Brands

Millennials are better-informed consumers than Boomers or Generation Xers were at an early age. They don't have to rely on experts or even brands to make choices, because they grew up tapping the Internet-empowered wisdom of crowds (think of star ratings on Amazon or TripAdvisor). They typically visit more than ten sources of online information before buying.[20] Their comfort with applications employing big data makes them open to customized comparison shopping.

Marketers often talk about a product's "features and benefits," and there's a subtle but significant difference in what generations value. Whereas Boomers tend to look at features and quality inherent in a product (or an institution), Millennials tend to look at benefits and experiences.[21] In other words, they look past a product and ask, "What will it *feel like* to own this device . . . or go to this college? What is the experiential return for my investment of time and money? How will this change me for the better?"

They have a unique perspective on what constitutes quality in a product or service. If Boomers and Generation X grew up with IBM and Microsoft as their respective models, Millennials grew up with the ethos of Apple and Google, and Generation Z grew up with the disruptive examples of Uber and Airbnb. As consumers, for example, they gravitate toward products that feature a high level of design, whether in electronics (smartphones), big-ticket items (cars), or even coffee (Starbucks). They are at the forefront of the consumer trend that values experiences over things, and access over ownership (using Uber and Zipcar as opposed to owning an automobile).[22] That these trends do not yet dominate the economy doesn't mean they won't grow as these generations account for more and more spending.

Expect even more pressure for institutions to justify the cost of an education beyond simple postgraduate salary or job placement data. The Gallup-Purdue study cited earlier is prescient on this: students will judge a college's value based on how satisfied its graduates are with their overall sense of well-being—not just on their financial security or social status.

Institutions like American University have responded to this by studying customer-obsessed companies like Wegman's, a grocery store chain and perennial winner of "best of the best" awards. American's initiative, called Reinventing the Student Experience (RiSE), is a long-term plan to better service student needs, from campus communication to curriculum design. To be clear: The university is not compromising academic standards in an effort to "please customers." Rather, RiSE is designed to make the experience of attending American better and more individual for an ever more diverse student population.[23]

Recommendations: Become more specific about the experience of attending a particular college, as opposed to eventual outcomes. Spell out the benefits that students will reap for their investment and how students will feel before, during, and after their college years. Because many hard skills will be useful in the postgraduation world for only a limited amount of time, emphasize (and prove) that the college experience will prepare a student mentally and emotionally to manage change. And adapt to a crowdsourced world—enlist students to advocate for the school on social media with authentic, voluntary, and narrative testimony.

They Are Socially Conscious and Dedicated to Improving the World

Of everything we learned about Millennials in the PreparedU survey, this is the most gratifying point to me. As a group, they are committed to the triple bottom line: people, planet, and profit. Fully 95 percent of Millennials said that a company's ethics are very important to them in choosing where to work. And although other generations want to work and shop at companies that demonstrate social and environmental commitment, Millennials make this part of their consumer identities. Eighty-nine percent say they are more likely to buy products and services from socially responsible companies.[24] Moreover, they want others to follow suit, as evidenced by their high rate of sharing information about those companies on social media.

> As a group, they are committed to the triple bottom line: people, planet, and profit. Fully 95 percent of Millennials said that a company's ethics are very important to them in choosing where to work.

Stories of these generations' idealism are among my favorites to tell incoming first-year students. I like to tell them about Maddie Bulkely, who graduated four years ago with a double major in marketing and liberal studies.

Her passion for food that is good for people and the environment led Bulkely to the liberal studies earth, environment, and global sustainability concentration; she also raised campus awareness of sustainability issues through the student-organized Eco-Reps program.

The summer after her junior year, Bulkely landed an internship with Quinn Popcorn—a young company with Boston roots, producing the first chemical-free microwave popcorn packaged in compostable bags. Bulkely's marketing smarts and belief in the company's values prompted Quinn to extend her internship through senior year; then the company hired her full-time. Bulkely's title at Quinn is "natural sales manager," and she relocated with the company to Boulder, Colorado, in 2014.

Another example is alumnus Tom D'Eri 2011, cofounder and chief operating officer for Rising Tide Car Wash. The Florida-based company's mission is to hire people with autism spectrum disorder, which affects some 3.5 million Americans—one of whom is Tom's brother, Andrew. Eight months of research led Tom to the car wash industry for its scalability, consumer-facing nature, and expansion potential. His judgment proved spot-on: Rising Tide began turning a profit in only seven months. Tom's larger aim is social change. He has shared the Rising Tide story in national media, business settings, and other venues, in hopes of redefining autism as a diversity with real value in the workplace.

Seeking out employers committed to social responsibility and innovation reflects Millennials' own entrepreneurial spirit. They want to innovate and create change with the work they do. We found that when Millennials evaluate whether they might want to work at a company, they tune in to the ethical dimension of the company culture. Unfortunately, their expectations are low: fewer Millennials (49 percent) than non-Millennials (70 percent) say that people in business do the right thing when faced with a tough decision.

They are influencers, not radicals. Walter Frick of *Harvard Business Review* captured their attitude well when he wrote, "Today's younger workers aren't seeking a revolution. They're too practical for that. Instead, they're taking jobs in corporate America and, in the process, insisting that average companies clean up their act."[25]

Recommendations: Connect values and professional skills from the first day students step onto campus—in the classroom, in the career center, in mentoring, in service-learning. Business curricula should teach the triple bottom line: the measurable benefit of business practices to people, planet, and profit. Problem sets must include a solution's ethical consequences, and institutions must be open to quantifying success in more than material terms—with data and an openness to differing views of what constitutes a social good.

They Are Poised to Change the Workplace

Roll up the changes in technology, economy, and business practices, and it becomes clear that Millennials and Generation Z are primed to change the workplace.

Unhelpful myths about Millennials and Generation Z at work persist. Loyalty to employers is a particular sore point for business. In Bentley's PreparedU survey, half of business professionals (51 percent) and more than half of Millennials (58 percent) agreed that businesses tend to think of Millennials as dispensable—just another employee who will be gone in a few years—and thus don't invest in their career development. Why should we improve your skills, companies say, only to see you take them to a competitor? The Great Recession cut company training and professional development budgets, and the suspicion about training people who will then leave for a better offer has held those investments back in many companies since the recovery began.

When you consider the costs and benefits of developing employees, this attitude is revealed as shortsighted. Raising an existing employee's skill set typically costs less than hiring a new worker; the price tag to replace an employee who quits is 50 percent to 150 percent of an annual salary.[26]

Today's graduates offer an opportunity to change that, because they have different expectations of how to acquire skills. Instead of higher-cost corporate classrooms, companies can make flexible arrangements including online training, offering incentives for completing training or achieving new competencies. They can adopt advanced methods and expertise from business schools. With the hybrid model in mind, they can fill skill gaps of high-potential employees, so as to make changing departments or functions a promising alternative to changing companies. One way to deal with a shortage of a particular skill set is to hire it in, but another way is to create it within the existing employee base. The latter way is getting less expensive thanks to educational technology, and the open, adaptable, and intellectually adventurous mind-set of today's graduates makes this an attractive way to stay ahead of skills shortages.

After about 2011, as the recovery continued, some companies anticipated the competition for top talent and proactively brought support back to the workplace. My friend Jerry Sargent, a top executive at Citizens Bank, told me that his company reintroduced training and support when they discovered they were wrong about Millennials and loyalty. Jerry says, "We discovered that the Millennial generation tends to seek alignment with companies who communicate clear career path opportunities, provide an infrastructure of support and connectivity to other areas of our company so they can be mobile, and encourage engagement on important social issues that impact our community."

When companies are loyal to the new generation of employees (giving training as well as opportunities to grow and advance), they are just as likely to stay as prior generations.

It is a myth that Millennial employees are by their natures disloyal and that they're going to move on if executives and managers aren't taking care of them properly. Bentley's PreparedU survey found that 55 percent of Millennials felt loyal to the company they worked for—but just over half (51 percent) did not expect loyalty from the company.[27] Although the Bureau of Labor Statistics continues to observe that job tenure is getting shorter, 16 percent in our survey told us that they'll stay with their current employer for the rest of their career!

Social consciousness does not mean that today's students and recent graduates are selfless. In the PreparedU survey, 79 percent of respondents expect a pay raise every year. Maybe that attitude is the genesis of the "entitled" complaint, but I think it might also reflect their emerging self-confidence (and perhaps a more assertive attitude about money, after the challenges of the last decade).[28]

Another rap on younger graduates is that they have a less than sterling work ethic, and this belief is not exclusive to older managers. In 2014, the PreparedU survey found that the number one reason Millennials cited for being unprepared was a poor work ethic.

Where did that perception come from? According to Leslie Doolittle, assistant dean and director of academic support services at Bentley, it stems from a difference in how younger and older generations view work.

"While older generations think of their job as a large part of who they are, today's graduates see work as a piece of their life but not everything," says Doolittle. "In other words, work doesn't define them. Family, friends, and making a difference in their community are much more central to them than previous generations." As a result, Millennials seek to have more work-life balance. "Frankly," says Doolittle, "I see this as a healthy adjustment to our worldview of work."

Growing up in an accelerated, on-demand world, these generations sometimes expect everyone around them to be working on the same fast track. Their aspirational views can be seen as entitled, and their agility can be misunderstood as overconfidence. The onus is on all of us—every generation—to work harder to understand each other and adapt to different work styles.

This attitude also reflects their flexibility around work hours. Millennials and Generation Z employees will head outside at 5 p.m. to play rugby, and then return to work to finish a project at 10 p.m. or later that night. They want employers to give them flexibility and then hold them accountable for results, and many employers can do this where appropriate.

> When work, play, and community are not separate but one continuous stream of interaction, employees are open to new connections.
>
> Organizations that embrace the qualities that distinguish these generations will gain tremendous value.

Millennial and Generation Z's "impatience" is a temperamental extension of living in an instant-feedback world, and it's healthy for business and educators alike to take a look at how the Millennial and Generation Z experience can encourage a new attitude. When work, play, and community are not separate but one continuous stream of interaction, employees are open to new connections. Organizations that embrace the qualities that distinguish these generations will gain tremendous value.

Recommendations: Equip today's students to adapt to their workplaces by understanding (and not rejecting) the habits of earlier generations. Teach a new concept of loyalty as a trusted set of relationships and behaviors, rather than as a lifelong transactional exchange of work for money. Train business professionals who will act as mentors knowledgeable in the differences among generations, and seek out those who advocate cooperation and mutual respect among generations.

Hybrid learning as I've described it is founded in the understanding that life after graduation has changed so much in recent years that higher education must adjust. There is a larger principle at work here as well, a simple, rather old-fashioned principle that can get lost in the scramble to keep on top of radical changes: all generations are in this together. Our work as educators is to encourage creative solutions that accept the twin facts that change is difficult for people and institutions and that adaptation is necessary to survival. And because we're all in this together, we owe it to each other—every generation— to listen and to learn what each generation has to teach.

Millennial and Generation Z Women

When I graduated Vassar, change was in the air: in 1970, Gloria Steinem had delivered a landmark address for the Vassar commencement, titled "Living the Revolution," which debunked prevalent myths about gender differences. Vassar was just going coeducational.

In 1970, 55 percent of male high school graduates and 48.5 percent of female high school graduates went on to attend some form of higher education. By 2014, women high school grads had leaped past men, with graduate enrollment rates of 72.6 percent (female) and 64.0 percent (male).[29] Today, women outnumber men in enrollment across ethnic and economic strata. Another way to look at women's dominance of higher education is to view total college enrollment by sex. According to the US Census Bureau, women outnumbered men attending two-year, four-year, and graduate programs 56 percent to 44 percent.[30]

That's not the case in business school, however, where men outnumber women 53 percent to 47 percent.[31] There are many reasons that fewer women choose to major in business, including the daunting news that year after year, in ways subtle and obvious, they don't receive the same opportunities as men.

> Girls might be interested in business, but less inclined to make the commitment to a school that focuses on business education, even one with an advanced hybrid model merging business and liberal arts.

Business schools need to find new ways to encourage more women to apply, and see to it that they thrive in their college years. One of the challenges we face attracting female undergraduates is that girls at sixteen and seventeen years of age are just not sure what to do with their lives. (The same is true for boys.) They look to role models in family, community, and media for guidance, and even today, many of these sources encourage boys more than girls to consider business careers. Girls might be interested in business, but less inclined to make the commitment to a school that focuses on business education, even one with an advanced hybrid model merging business and liberal arts. Admissions and marketing teams at Bentley and other colleges with strong undergraduate business programs should expend greater effort and find innovative ways to locate these "undecided-but-interested" young women and make their case.

Business schools must also address the "confidence gap" better than they have in the past. Since 2009, the management consultancy Bain & Company has studied the ways in which women's career paths differ from men's, and its periodic reports hold fascinating insights. Among its findings: 43 percent of women aspire to top management in the first two years of their position in a company, but after about two years, that number drops to 16 percent. Men's aspirations stay steady during those years at 34 percent. As women gain experience, their confidence diminishes by half. One Bain report states the origin of this plainly: "Only 30% of women in middle management and 24% of women in upper management and executive positions believe there is an equal opportunity to be promoted on the same timeline as men, compared with 51% and 46%, respectively, of their male counterparts."[32]

Bain, a company famously driven by hard data, points out the cost of this gender disparity. Its numbers show that companies where employees believe that women and men have equal opportunity have higher employee engagement scores than companies where employees believe that the sexes do not have the same opportunity. Employee engagement, roughly meaning the degree to which employees voluntarily go "above and beyond" the minimum effort required, is a key indicator of positive business outcomes.[33]

It seems that the Baby Boomers and Generation X, who are senior managers today, haven't solved this problem. Women's voices are still not being heard. Women aren't being sponsored, and they are not being developed and prepared for larger roles, and they see it. Good intentions are not enough. Training is not enough, because at least 70 percent of leadership development occurs on the job, where high-potential employees are given high-profile assignments and opportunities to lead.[34]

Related to this is the "impostor syndrome," that struggle many women go through when they first take on a leadership position. It's the feeling that no matter what you have accomplished, despite all tangible evidence to the contrary, you can't quite believe that you deserve your success. For this, the best remedy is early intervention by a mentor. Very early in my career, at the Federal Trade Commission, a barrier-breaking woman named Patricia Bailey (see chapter 4) not only served as a role model for me but also encouraged and assisted me to move into leadership roles. Although my impostor syndrome was not erased entirely, her belief in me and her practical advice added to my self-confidence.

We have a long way to go. General population surveys show lingering sex-role stereotypes when it comes to career expectations.[35] Yet, once again, I am encouraged by the special characteristics of Millennials and Generation Z.

One reason for optimism is that these students and graduates are less bound by tradition. All that impatience and skepticism people talk about has an upside—they question tradition, including embedded inequality. Their technical acumen is empowering. They are used to tweaking, changing, customizing, and challenging everything in their lives, from consumer choices to social media feeds. Their loyalty must be earned and re-earned, and if that seems like a bad thing, consider the importance of that attitude to innovation and creative destruction. In a positive sense, these students and recent graduates won't accept the status quo.

Here's what I've observed firsthand: their attitude toward unequal opportunity is a frank and unequivocal rejection of such prejudice. They might be the ones who finally batter down the walls of discrimination, especially against women in business.

How can business education leverage these attitudes? How can we prepare women (and men) to make a world of equal opportunity?

There's no doubt that a majority of CEOs want to promote equality. They don't need more proof that it's the right thing to do as well as the most profitable thing to do in the long run. But over and over, well-intentioned programs in corporations fail to move the needle in the right direction. Corporate leaders are not looking for the *why* of gender equality; they want to find the *how*.

> It's progress for women to be heard in the boardroom, but until they are really heard in the meeting room, at the project level, and at the middle-management level, the dismal advancement figures won't change much.

Bentley's Center for Women and Business (CWB) explores the action steps that can be taken in education and business to move women into positions of leadership. It is dedicated to following conversation with action. We teach outside corporate partners in such areas as men in partnership, how to build a sponsorship program, how to learn gender intelligence, and how to deal with flex time. There are so many things a company can do if finding and developing talented women is a top-line priority. But although the work of changing culture starts at the top, it has to pervade the company at all levels. Yes, it's progress for women to be heard in the boardroom, but until they are really heard in the meeting room, at the project level, and at the middle-management level, the dismal advancement figures won't change much.

A lot of today's male graduates heard their fathers say, "I regret not being around while my kids were little." They saw their mothers throttle back on work commitments to take on most of child care and household management. They don't want that kind of life, in part because they see their female peers as equals, and in part because they blur the lines between work life and home or community life.

This is promising, and it raises an even greater challenge to corporate America than the questions of equal pay and equal opportunity: the challenge of designing a successful business career that doesn't require a manager or executive to put business first and everything else second. Millennials and Generation Z have the potential to work more flexibly because they know how to focus on results. They are less attached than previous generations to "how it's always been done."

The CWB offers a practical template for women to prepare for work after graduation. Although the advice is applicable to men as well, the template specifically addresses the gaps that we notice in female business students' preparation. It consists of five key skills based on the hybrid work model:

1. Establish a set of hard, quantifiable skills, which are essential in landing a first job. Examples include computer programming, web design, nursing, finance, accounting, writing, and engineering.

2. At the same time, develop soft skills that are necessary to advancing a career. These include work ethic, communication skills, self-awareness, and other qualities discussed in chapter 3.

3. Learn to tell your story. From impressing a manager in a behavior-based interview to inspiring confidence in a

mentor, a clear narrative has unequaled impact. Women are trained from an early age to be self-effacing, and many self-censor when it comes to common business situations like taking credit or proposing a plan. We train women to demonstrate their positive impact on business by quantifying the results of their work.

4. Be tough on stereotypes. You know what I'm talking about: "Don't be bossy." "Don't you care about your family?" "Don't be so [ambitious, tough, exacting, etc.]." The skill of assertive self-awareness and permission to use it have to be normalized by women if they're to succeed. Calling out stereotypes and explicitly disproving them also engenders personal resilience, which anyone in business needs, but women especially have to cultivate.

5. Know the business inside and out. This is obviously part of the mission of a business university; for young women, it means learning to seek out influencers, mentors, sponsors, and insiders in addition to professors. Everyone needs a personal "brain trust" to help her analyze and understand her chosen field. Today's students have the advantage of incredible research skills as well as a global outlook, and we strive to help them use those to construct powerful professional networks before they graduate.

The CWB is focused on preparing women for every stage of their careers. We create programming to help women succeed at every level. We bring in men and women from the C-suite and corporate boards to talk about their career paths. We get female executives and middle managers to talk about their early-stage development—where they succeeded or failed.

We work directly with faculty in the classroom, as well as with companies, so that students never lose sight of the real world.

And there's one other thing we do, which is to bring in men to participate in the women's programs. I'm particularly proud of that, because it's the piece that my generation of women forgot. "Oh yeah, there should be guys at the table too."

The table has room for guys. And gals. And Boomers, Generation X, Millennials, and Generation Z. We all can learn from one another, if we're willing to listen. Today's students fill me with optimism because they are ready to step up to the table with energy, enthusiasm, and open minds. Educators and business leaders together must make it a priority to prepare them for the world of ever-accelerating change. It is the world that we made that they inherit and that they can change for good.

AFTERWORD

In February 1917, Harry C. Bentley founded the Bentley school of Accounting and Finance in a single room at 30 Huntington Avenue in Boston. Having taught at Boston University and other area schools, Bentley saw an opportunity to go beyond traditional bookkeeping and introduce his own, more sophisticated accountancy training. Confirming his belief in his methods, thirty former students enrolled in his school and called themselves the Bentley Associates.

It was a formative time in professional education. Business schools at Harvard, University of Chicago, University of California, MIT, and Dartmouth were all less than twenty years old. In 1917, the first national standardized test to certify CPAs was introduced by the American Institute of Certified Public Accountants.[1]

World War I and the years immediately following it stand as an inflexion point for business and education. According to the Economic History Association, the 1920s "marks the first truly modern decade . . . The period saw major innovations in business organization and manufacturing technology."[2] Automobile ownership exploded. Vast new networks of electricity ended the isolation of the most far-flung homes. Commercial radio's debut heralded the advent of nationwide electronic media. New forms of entertainment—professional sports, movies, inexpensive home music players—all swelled in popularity.

Does all this sound familiar? A century later, global economies are undergoing changes just as sweeping. Innovation in every field, from manufacturing to big data, challenges business leaders to compete or to engage in creative destruction whereby new technologies and business models remake entire industries. Incalculable amounts of information pass through financial systems daily. The Internet puts the worldwide media into anyone's hand. Business and other careers have become a mosaic of engagements requiring people to integrate left- and right-brain skills. Like Harry Bentley, we are living an inflexion point in economic, social, and cultural history.

Those who educate tomorrow's leaders can take a lesson from the pioneers who changed business education a century ago: when innovation creates dynamic economies and new social norms, higher education must also innovate. This is not a retrenchment but a huge opportunity.

In this book, I've reviewed a number of ways that campus-based hybrid learning models are answering the challenge of our new century. As a college president for ten years, I worked to convene voices of change across the initiative we call PreparedU at Bentley University. We put forth our ideas and practices and listened eagerly to others. We experimented, measured the results, and integrated the best of what we learned into the college experience.

Ours is not the only model; it offers one wide-ranging set of principles and practical steps for educators, parents, students, policymakers, and others to meet the challenge of rapidly changing demands from the world of work. The pillars of a new educational experience—academic excellence, technology training, hands-on learning, career skills, and service-learning—are a foundation for many approaches.

We are already seeing progress. The business community believes today that graduates are better prepared for work and life than they were just a few years ago. Follow-on surveys from our initial PreparedU research show growing consensus between business and educators as to what's needed.

The more successful, larger, and richer schools have a special obligation to lead and share what they learn. For example, when we at Bentley learned that smaller colleges and smaller employers were finding it difficult to construct robust internship programs, Bentley's associate VP of career services, Susan Brennan, stepped up to help design an online service for matching students and opportunities. In partnership with the Greater Boston Chamber of Commerce, the Boston Fed, and others, Bentley developed and rolled out the service to other colleges and small employers free of charge.

> If educational technology can promote the success factors that Gallup-Purdue's research confirmed—factors that are ultimately grounded in strong human relationships, self-knowledge, and open minds—then it will be a huge benefit to individuals and the institutions that serve them.

There are incredible new tools and techniques entering all domains of education. Advances in big data and artificial intelligence are just beginning to infiltrate the nontechnical college experience. Choices ranging from which college to attend, to which internships to pursue, to which major to study, are going to get a lot more interesting as data analysis and personal assessments reveal hidden opportunities for every student based on his or her skills, temperament, values, and life experiences. Colleges should welcome this next wave of progress even though it will require considerable adjustment to their internal and external systems (of recruiting, financial aid, and even curriculum), because the result will be a greater number of students accessing the right education, in the right form, in the right place, at the right time. If educational technology can promote the success factors that Gallup-Purdue's research confirmed—factors that are ultimately grounded in strong human relationships, self-knowledge, and open minds—then it will be a huge benefit to individuals and the institutions that serve them. In the context of hybrid learning, these technologies do not limit choice but empower students of any age to make better choices for themselves.

We have been through some tough times. The global recession of 2008–2009 and its slow recovery left many young graduates financially adrift for years. The members of the "barista generation" of underemployed, overindebted graduates are statistically behind their younger brothers and sisters in their career advancement. One question for policymakers to tackle now is how to help them catch up without disadvantaging the next generation.

My ten years at the helm of a business university gives me great confidence in the ability of Millennials and Generation Z. As a group they are confident, outspoken, hardworking, and globally minded. Older generations should celebrate those differences as Millennials and Generation Z increase their already-majority status in the workplace. I hope they continue to embrace the attitudes I saw when they were students: raising their hands to take on more responsibility, ask how to help, share ideas, or serve their communities. I hope they continue to share their unique and informed perspective to recommend solutions to business, economic, social, and global problems. I hope they continue to be the "can do" generations with the energy to embrace work *and* play, career *and* service, community *and* individual achievement. Their holistic approach to work and life deserves a holistic approach to higher education, not only because it suits them but also because it suits the twenty-first century.

The world is not going back to a time when you didn't have to consider how your education will give you all the tools you'll need in society before you graduate. It's not 1970 anymore; the luxury of postponing career-oriented education that was granted to so many in my generation is gone. Students and their families are looking for a college experience that combines left-brain and right-brain skills. They need skills to manage work and life that will grow in scope and sophistication long beyond the day they graduate. They deserve an education the reflects the innovation economy: creativity *and* analytic acumen, emotional intelligence *and* critical thinking.

It was my hope when I came to Bentley University that I could help these amazing young people prepare for the unprecedented demands of the innovation economy. After ten years, I am gratified to see examples around the country (and the world) of higher education changing to meet those demands. I hope that this book, gathering many voices from colleagues, students, businesspeople, and policymakers, contributes further to that progress.

—*Gloria Cordes Larson*

ENDNOTES

Introduction

1. Thomas Friedman, *The World Is Flat: A Brief History of the Twenty-First Century*, 2nd ed. (New York: Farrar, Straus & Giroux, 2005), 570.

2. James Brice, "Globalization Comes to Radiology," DiagnosticImaging.com (CMP Healthcare Media, November 2003), http://web.mit.edu/outsourcing/class1/ DI-radiology-1.htm. For law, see www.pangea3.com.

3. Josh Bersin, "Spending on Corporate Training Soars: Employee Capabilities Now a Priority," *Forbes,* February 4, 2014, http://www.forbes.com/sites/joshbersin/2014/02/04/ the-recovery-arrives-corporate-training-spend-skyrockets/ #53ca6da94ab7. Training budgets began to increase in 2010, and are now significantly higher.

4. Pink cautions that his book is not a medical textbook, and I repeat the point here. The left-brain and right-brain groupings of skills are an effective metaphor, not precise neurological science.

5. Friedman has since added items to the list, most urgently global climate change and population growth.

6. Bentley University Office of Career Services. Data as of the class of 2015.

7. Carly Stockwell, "Same as It Ever Was: Top 10 Most Popular College Majors," *USA Today,* October 26, 2014, http://college.usatoday.com/2014/10/26/same-as-it-ever-was-top-10-most-popular-college-majors/.

8. National Center for Education Statistics, "Fast Facts," Tables 322.10 and 323.10, https://nces.ed.gov/fastfacts/display.asp?id=37.

Chapter 1

1. Pew Research Center, "The Rising Cost of Not Going to College" (February 11, 2014), http://www.pcwsocial-trends.org/2014/02/11/the-rising-cost-of-not-going-to-college/. According to the Pew Research Center, median earnings for workers with a bachelor's degree in 2013 were 62 percent higher those of workers with only a high school education.

2. Harvard Law School, "Admissions FAQ" (n.d.), http://hls.harvard.edu/dept/jdadmissions/apply-to-harvard-law-school/the-application-process/admissions-faq/#faq-1-6.

3. Valerie Calderon, "Maximize the Return on Your Investment in Higher Education," *Gallup Blog,* July 22, 2015, http://www.gallup.com/opinion/gallup/184286/maximize-return-investment-higher-education.aspx.

4. The term *college* in this book indicates all accredited postsecondary institutions: colleges, universities, state schools, and graduate schools.

5. Frank Bruni, *Where You Go Is Not Who You'll Be: An Antidote to the College Admissions Mania* (New York: Grand Central Publishing, 2015).

6. Megan Elliott, "CEOs Who Didn't Pursue Undergrad Business Degrees," *USA Today,* March 29, 2015, http://www.usatoday.com/story/money/business/2015/03/29/cheat-sheet-ceos-college-business/70442270/. Also Sarah J. Mitchell, "Remaining Hope for the Liberal Arts Degree: Fortune 500 CEO's Who Have Read the Classics," *Taglines* (blog), Alexander Group, January 27, 2014, https://www.thealexandergroup.com/blog-press-room/2014/major-humanities-ceos/.

7. Gallup, *Great Jobs Great Lives: The 2014 Gallup-Purdue Index Report* (2014), https://www.luminafoundation.org/files/resources/galluppurdueindex-report-2014.pdf, 6.

8. Julie Ray and Stephanie Kafka, "Life in College Matters for Life after College," Gallup, May 6, 2014, http://www.gallup.com/poll/168848/life-college-matters-life-college.aspx.

9. Cathie Gandel, "Business Schools Give Undergraduate Programs a Liberal Arts Twist," *U.S. News Education,* September 9, 2015, http://www.usnews.com/education/best-colleges/articles/2015/09/09/business-schools-give-undergraduate-programs-a-liberal-arts-twist.

Chapter 2

1. Mary C. Daly and Leila Bengali, "Is It Still Worth Going to College?" *FRBSF Economic Letter,* May 5, 2014, https://www.luminafoundation.org/files/resources/el2014-13.pdf.

2. Burning Glass, *Moving the Goalposts: How Demand for a Bachelor's Degree Is Reshaping the Workforce* (September 2014), http://burning-glass.com/wp-content/uploads/Moving_the_Goalposts.pdf.

3. Circuit City, Pitney Bowes, and Fannie Mae.

4. Jim Collins, "Good to Great to Gone," *Economist*, July 7, 2009, http://www.economist.com/node/13980976.

5. Sweet Briar College almost shut down for financial reasons in 2015; only an extraordinary fundraising effort by alumnae and others prevented the shutdown. Susan Svrluga, "Supporters to Make Final Payment to Sweet Briar College, with a Little Extra Thrown In," *Washington Post*, September 2, 2015, https://www.washingtonpost.com/news/grade-point/wp/2015/09/01/supporters-to-make-final-payment-to-sweet-briar-college-with-a-little-extra-thrown-in/?utm_term=.002c7cade4ef.

6. 2016 rankings, *Wall Street Journal* and *Forbes*, respectively.

7. Jonathan Rothwell and Siddharth Kulkarni, "Beyond College Rankings: A Value-Added Approach to Assessing Two- and Four-Year Schools," Brookings Institution, https://www.brookings.edu/wp-content/uploads/2015/04/BMPP_CollegeValueAdded.pdf. Two notes on this study are worth considering: (1) The ranking includes maritime and pharmaceutical schools. Their earnings data skew higher within ten years of graduation, but the long-term payoff is less. (2) The data used in this study comes from College Scorecard, which means that respondents are only individuals with federal student loans.

8. Emily Gera, "World of Warcraft Players Are the Ideal Employee, Says John Seely Brown," *Polygon*, January 3, 2013, http://www.polygon.com/2013/1/3/3831408/world-of-warcraft-players-are-the-ideal-employee-says-john-seely-brown.

9. "State of the MOOC 2016: A Year of Massive Landscape Change for Massive Open Online Courses," *Online Course Report* (2016), https://www.onlinecoursereport.com/state-of-the-mooc-2016-a-year-of-massive-landscape-change-for-massive-open-online-courses/.

10. Frederic Lardinois, "Coursera Raises $49.5M Series C Funding Led by NEA, Expects Second Closing Will Bring Total to $60M," *TechCrunch,* August 25, 2015, https://techcrunch.com/2015/08/25/coursera-raises-49-5m-series-c-funding-led-by-nea-expects-second-closing-will-bring-total-to-60m/.

11. Julia Bell, "Penn Is Offering an Online Course about How to Apply to College," *Daily Pennsylvanian,* November 21, 2016, http://www.thedp.com/article/2016/11/penn-admissions-online-course.

12. Gallup, *Great Jobs Great Lives: The 2014 Gallup-Purdue Index Report* (2014), https://www.luminafoundation.org/files/resources/galluppurdueindex-report-2014.pdf.

Chapter 3

1. Meredith Mason, "Bentley on Bloomberg: The Extended Classroom," *PreparedU View,* October 20, 2016, http://www.bentley.edu/prepared/bentley-on-bloomberg-extended-classroom.

2. Jack Zenger and Joseph Folkman, "The Skills Leaders Need at Every Level," *Harvard Business Review*, July 30, 2014, https://hbr.org/2014/07/the-skills-leaders-need-at-every-level.

3. The PreparedU Project, January 2014. The surveys included a multiphase approach including quantitative

and qualitative interviews, a literature review, and a survey of 3,149 individuals, answering more than three hundred questions. I'll return to its findings throughout this book.

4. *Do Today's Graduates Have the Skills They Need to Succeed?* (2016), report by Bentley University and Anderson Robbins Research, https://www.bentley.edu/files/2016/09/16/preparedu-executive-summary.pdf.

5. Ibid.

6. Tony Wagner and Ted Dintersmith, *Most Likely to Succeed: Preparing Our Kids for the Innovation Era* (New York: Scribner, 2015), 223.

7. Peter Drucker, "Managing Oneself," *Harvard Business Review,* 1999. Available as Reprint R0501K from *Harvard Business Review* at https://hbr.org/2005/01/managing-oneself.

8. Bentley University, "Bentley University's PreparedU Project: Millennials in the Workplace Infographic Storybook," *in SlideShare,* https://www.slideshare.net/BentleyU/prepared-u-project-millennials-in-the-workplace.

9. Association of American Colleges and Universities, "Falling Short? College Learning and Career Success: National Surveys of Business and Nonprofit Leaders and Current College Students" (2015), https://www.aacu.org/leap/public-opinion-research/2015-survey-falling-short.

10. Laszlo Bock, *Work Rules! Insights from Google That Will Transform How You Live and Lead* (New York: Hachette, 2015), 99–100. I'll add that Bock and Google generally hold out for supercandidates, but they can afford to— they get more than 2 million job applications a year!

11. Frank Bruni, "College's Priceless Value," *New York Times*, February 11, 2015, https://www.nytimes.com/2015/02/11/opinion/frank-bruni-higher-education-liberal-arts-and-shakespeare.html.

12. Bock, *Work Rules!*

13. Quentin Hardy, "Gearing Up for the Cloud, AT&T Tells Its Workers: Adapt, or Else." *New York Times*, February 14, 2016, https://www.nytimes.com/2016/02/14/technology/gearing-up-for-the-cloud-att-tells-its-workers-adapt-or-else.html.

14. Lora Kolodny, "Coursera Expands into Corporate Learning and Development," *TechCrunch*, August 31, 2016, https://techcrunch.com/2016/08/31/coursera-expands-into-corporate-learning-and-development/.

15. Emily Caruthers, "Is Uber Crushing the Taxi Industry?" *CNBC.com*, March 3, 2015, http://www.cnbc.com/2015/03/03/is-uber-crushing-the-taxi-industry.html.

16. The notion of an innovation economy was introduced by economist Joseph Schumpeter in 1942. Schumpeter also introduced the core ideas of creative destruction; it took decades for these ideas to become common knowledge.

17. Eric E. Schmidt, "The Courage to Be Unreasonable" (Penn commencement address), *Almanac* 55, no. 34 (May 26, 2009), http://www.upenn.edu/almanac/volumes/v55/n34/comm-schmidt.html. Accessed January 12, 2017.

18. Bradley Johnson, "What You Need to Know about the Global Ad Market," *AdAge*, December 8, 2014, http://adage.com/article/global-news/global-ad-market/296104/.

19. Statista, "Google's Ad Revenue from 2001 to 2016 (in Billion U.S. Dollars)," https://www.statista.com/statistics/266249/advertising-revenue-of-google/.

20. Dan Frommer, "Amazon Web Services Is Approaching a $10-Billion-a-Year Business," *Re/Code,* April 28, 2016, http://www.recode.net/2016/4/28/11586526/aws-cloud-revenue-growth.

21. *Work Rules!* describes innovations Bock made at every step in the hiring process, from attraction to making offers.

22. Bentley University, "Future-Proof Your Career: Why You Need Left and Right Brain Skills for Tomorrow's Jobs," February 16, 2016, https://www.slideshare.net/BentleyU/futureproof-your-career-58330605. Research done by Burning Glass for Bentley University's PreparedU project.

23. Joseph E. Aoun, "Hybrid Jobs Call for Hybrid Educations," *Harvard Business Review,* April 12, 2016, https://hbr.org/2016/04/hybrid-jobs-call-for-hybrid-education.

24. Thomas Friedman, "Donald Trump Voters, Just Hear Me Out," *New York Times,* November 2, 2016, https://www.nytimes.com/2016/11/02/opinion/donald-trump-voters-just-hear-me-out.html.

25. Bruni, "College's Priceless Value."

26. Millennial generation expert Lindsey Pollack points out that Generation Xers tend to be least tolerant of the differences that Millennials present—almost like a generational sibling rivalry. How this will all get sorted out in the workplace will be one of the big stories of management in the coming decades.

27. Deloitte, *Mind the Gaps: The 2015 Deloitte Millennial Survey; Executive Summary,* https://www2.deloitte .com/content/dam/Deloitte/global/Documents /About-Deloitte/gx-wef-2015-millennial-survey-executivesummary.pdf.

28. In the United States, women slightly outpolled men in terms of their "leadership" self-assessment.

Chapter 4

1. Hauserman is now an adjunct lecturer in management.

2. Michigan Ross, "The MERGE Curriculum" (2017), https://michiganross.umich.edu/programs/bba/ curriculum.

3. Olin College of Engineering, "At Olin the Culture Is the Curriculum" (n.d.), http://www.olin.edu/academics/ curriculum/.

4. US Department of Labor, Bureau of Labor Statistics, "Economic News Release," September 4, 2015, https:// www.bls.gov/opub/ted/2015/more-education-still-means-more-pay-in-2014.

5. Steven H. Woolf, Lauden Y. Aron, Lisa Dubay, Sarah M. Simon, Emily Zimmerman, and Kim Luk, *How Are Income and Wealth Linked to Health and Longevity?* Urban Institute, April 13, 2015. http://www.urban.org/ research/publication/how-are-income-and-wealth-linked-health-and-longevity/view/full_report. The reasons are complex, but the correlation is clear.

6. Six months after May 2014 graduation, 98 percent of Bentley graduates were either employed, attending

graduate school, or planning to attend graduate school. We've got that part right, but it doesn't diminish the need to work toward broader criteria.

7. Gallup, *Great Jobs Great Lives: The 2014 Gallup-Purdue Index Report* (2014), https://www.luminafoundation.org/files/resources/galluppurdueindex-report-2014.pdf.

8. Sava Berhané, "Why Women Need Career Sponsors More Than Mentors," *Fast Company,* August 28, 2015, https://www.fastcompany.com/3050430/strong-female-lead/why-women-need-career-sponsors-more-than-mentors.

9. Details taken from "Suze's Story" on www.suzeorman.com.

10. Meredith Mason, "Bentley on Bloomberg: How to Make the Most of the College Experience," May 23, 2016, http://www.bentley.edu/prepared/bentley-on-bloomberg-how-make-most-college-experience.

11. US Department of Labor, Bureau of Labor Statistics, "Employee Tenure Summary," September 18, 2014, http://www.bls.gov/news.release/tenure.nr0.htm.

12. I'll say more in chapter 6 about the importance of the cohort to the new model of hybrid learning.

13. Lauren Weber and Melissa Korn, "Where Did All the Entry-Level Jobs Go?" *Wall Street Journal,* August 6, 2014, https://www.wsj.com/articles/want-an-entry-level-job-youll-need-lots-of-experience-1407267498.

14. The issue of paid versus unpaid internships matters to the extent that students need the money for school, and it is an important factor in college-corporate partnership design.

15. Mark A. Hofmann, "Liberty Mutual's Thriving Internship Program Is a Valuable Hiring Resource," *Business Insurance,* August 22, 2012, http://www.businessinsurance.com/article/99999999/NEWS03/120829954/liberty-mutuals-thriving-internship-program-is-a-valuable-hiring-resource.

Chapter 5

1. Allison Dulin Salisbury, "Impacts of MOOCs on Higher Education: A Report from the UT Arlington Symposium," *Inside Higher Ed,* October 23, 2014, https://www.insidehighered.com/blogs/higher-ed-beta/impacts-moocs-higher-education.

2. A professor who made them excited about learning, professors who cared about them as a person, and a mentor who encouraged them to pursue their goals and dreams.

3. Shanell Mosley, "How Bentley Empowered Me to Make the World a Better Place," *The Biz,* September 16, 2016, http://thebiz.bentley.edu/bentley-empowered-make-world-better-place/.

4. NASPA is the organization of student affairs administrators in higher education.

5. Gallup, *Great Jobs. Great Lives. The Value of Career Services, Inclusive Experiences and Mentorship for College Graduates* (2016), https://www.luminafoundation.org/files/resources/great-jobs-great-livees-3-2016.pdf.

Chapter 6

1. Anne Colby, Thomas Ehrlich, William M. Sullivan, and Jonathan R. Dolle, *Rethinking Undergraduate Business Education: Liberal Learning for the Profession* (San Francisco: Jossey-Bass, 2011).

2. Lee S. Schulman, "Foreword," in Colby et al., *Rethinking Undergraduate Business Education,* xi.

3. Daniel L. Everett and Michael J. Page, "The Crucial Educational Fusion: Relevance, Rigor, and Life Preparation in a Changing World," in *Shaping the Future of Business Education,* ed. Gordon M. Hardy and Daniel L. Everett (Boston and London: Palgrave Macmillan, 2013), 1–16 (quotation on p. 4).

4. Catherine A. Usoff, "Integrating Liberal Learning into the Accounting Curriculum," in *Shaping the Future,* ed. Hardy and Everett, 61–71 (quotation on p. 64).

5. Christopher Beneke, "Change over Time: The Study of the Past and the Future of Business Education," in *Shaping the Future of Business Education,* ed. Hardy and Everett, 123–134.

6. Adam Connor-Simons, "New Undergrad Business Program among Most Popular," *Brandeis Now,* September 26, 2013, http://www.brandeis.edu/now/2013/september/business.html.

7. "New Dual Degree at WVU Injects Business Knowledge into Public Health," *WVU Today,* September 12, 2013, http://wvutoday.wvu.edu/n/2013/09/12/new-dual-degree-at-wvu-injects-business-knowledge-into-public-health.

8. Louis Lavelle, "Business Schools Embrace the Liberal Arts," *Bloomberg Business,* April 10, 2013, http://msb. georgetown.edu/newsroom/in-the-news/ business-schools-embrace-liberal-arts.

9. The six areas are arts/culture/creativity, transcultural or global experiences, undergraduate research, service-learning, leadership, and professional experience.

10. "Video Viewpoints: The College President's Take on Preparing Millennials for Work," *PreparedU View,* July 14, 2015, http://www.bentley.edu/prepared/ college-presidents-take-on-preparing-millennials-work-video.

11. The program, nicknamed 4DX, involves four hundred faculty, staff, and administrators. Its goal is to raise the performance of the colleges themselves. Its importance to the hybrid model is in the delivery of Alamo's services to its students.

12. "New Fusion Courses Make Unlikely Connections, Drive Creative Thinking," *PreparedU View,* June 18, 2014, http://www.bentley.edu/newsroom/latest-headlines/ new-fusion-courses-make-unlikely-connections-drive-creative-thinking.

13. Ian Cross, "It's Time Colleges Gave Students the Tools They Need to Get a Job," *PreparedU View,* April 17, 2015, http://www.bentley.edu/prepared/it%E2%80%99s-time-colleges-gave-students-tools-they-need-get-job.

14. Mark Frydenberg, "Digging Up Treasure in the CIS Sandbox," *PreparedU View* (n.d.), http://www.bentley. edu/impact/articles/digging-treasure-cis-sandbox.

Chapter 7

1. Starting and ending birth years for Millennials change depending on whom you ask. The US Census Bureau identifies only the Baby Boom generation (1946–1964) based on its clear demographic endpoint. I'm using Census Bureau data analyzed by the Pew Research Center, among others. As of now, Generation Z has no generally accepted demographic endpoint year, which means that the cited numbers are a conservative estimate. Also, this chapter is focused on those who have attended or are attending college.

2. Lindsey Pollak, *Becoming the Boss: New Rules for the Next Generation of Leaders* (New York: HarperCollins, 2014).

3. Richard Fry, "Millennials Overtake Baby Boomers as America's Largest Generation," Pew Research Center (April 25, 2016), http://www.pewresearch.org/fact-tank/2016/04/25/millennials-overtake-baby-boomers/. Numbers include immigration and deaths.

4. US Census Bureau, *The Next Four Decades* (May 2010), https://www.census.gov/prod/2010pubs/p25-1138.pdf.

5. "Myths, Exaggerations and Uncomfortable Truths: The Real Story behind Millennials in the Workplace," IBM Institute for Business Value (January 2015), https://www-935.ibm.com/services/us/gbs/thoughtleadership/millennialworkplace/.

6. Mary Meeker, *Internet Trends 2016—Code Conference,* Kleiner Perkins Caulfield Byers (June 1, 2016), http://www.kpcb.com/internet-trends.

7. For example, 27 percent of Millennial women and 21 percent of Millennial men hold bachelor's degrees, compared to an attainment rate for Boomers of

14 percent women, 17 percent men. Eileen Patten and Richard Fry, "How Millennials Today Compare with Their Grandparents 50 Years Ago," Pew Research Center (March 19, 2015), http://www.pewresearch.org/fact-tank/2015/03/19/how-millennials-compare-with-their-grandparents/.

8. Lisa B. Kahn, "The Long-Term Labor Market Consequences of Graduating from College in a Bad Economy," *Labour Economics* 17, no. 2 (2010): 303–316; see also "The Career Effects of Graduating in a Recession" (November 2006), http://www.nber.org/digest/nov06/w12159.html. The latter is a nontechnical summary of Philip Oreopoulos, Till von Wachter, and Andrew Heisz, "The Short- and Long-Term Career Effects of Graduating in a Recession: Hysteresis and Heterogeneity in the Market for College Graduates," National Bureau of Economic Research Working Paper No. 12159 (April 2006).

9. Council of Economic Advisors, "15 Economic Facts about Millennials" (October 2014), https://obamawhite-house.archives.gov/sites/default/files/docs/millennials_report.pdf. As of 2014, average real per-borrower debt was between $27,000 and $30,000.

10. Walter Frick, "Millennials Are Cynical Do-Gooders," *Harvard Business Review,* May 30, 2014. https://hbr.org/2014/05/millennials-are-cynical-do-gooders.

11. Anthony P. Carnevale, Andrew R. Hanson, and Artem Gulish, *Failure to Launch: Structural Shift and the New Lost Generation* (Washington DC: Georgetown University Center on Education and the Workforce), https://cew.georgetown.edu/cew-reports/failure-to-launch/.

12. Kevin Eagan, Ellen Bara Stolzenberg, Abigail K. Bates, Melissa C. Aragon, Maria Ramirez Suchard, and Cecilia Rios-Aguilar, *The American Freshman: National Norms 2015* (Los Angeles: Higher Education Research Institute, UCLA, 2015), https://www.heri.ucla.edu/monographs/TheAmericanFreshman2015.pdf.

13. Pew Research Center, "Millennials in Adulthood: Detached from Institutions, Networked with Friends" (March 7, 2014), http://www.pewsocialtrends.org/2014/03/07/millennials-in-adulthood/, 7-10.

14. Giselle Abramovich, "15 Mind-Blowing Stats about Generation Z," *CMO/Adobe,* June 12, 2015, http://www.cmo.com/features/articles/2015/6/11/15-mind-blowing-stats-about-generation-z.html#gs.=qs7IWU.

15. Pew Research Center, "Teens, Social Media and Technology Overview 2015" (April 9, 2015), http://www.pewinternet.org/2015/04/09/teens-social-media-technology-2015/, 5.

16. Julie Houpt and Bill Faust, "Engaging and Cultivating Millennials & Gen Z," *in SlideShare,* http://www.slideshare.net/Ologie/engaging-and-cultivating-millenials-gen-z.

17. Abramovich, "15 Mind-Blowing Stats."

18. Pew Research Center, "Social Networking Fact Sheet" (September 2014), http://www.pewinternet.org/fact-sheet/social-media/; Amanda Lenhart, "Teens, Social Media & Technology Overview, 2015," Pew Research Center (April 9, 2015), http://www.pewinternet.org/2015/04/09/teens-social-media-technology-2015/.

19. Pew Research Center, *Millennials in Adulthood: Detached from Institutions, Networked with Friends* (March 2014), 7. Report can be downloaded at http://www.pewsocial-trends.org/2014/03/07/millennials-in-adulthood/.

20. Thomas H. Davenport, "At the Big Data Crossroads: Turning toward a Smarter Travel Experience," Amadeus IT Group (2013), http://www.bigdata.amadeus.com/assets/pdf/Amadeus_Big_Data.pdf.

21. Kristen Baldwin, "Boomers vs. Millennials" (blog post), DMN3 Digital Marketing, April 29, 2015, https://www.dmn3.com/dmn3-blog/boomers-vs.-millennials-infographic.

22. Tracy Kosolcharoen, "Millennials: Fueling the Experience Economy," Eventbrite (2014), https://www.eventbrite.com/blog/academy/millennials-fueling-experience-economy/. According to an Eventbrite/Harris Interactive study, 78 percent of Millennials would choose to spend money on a desirable experience or event over buying something desirable.

23. Lee Gardner, "What a University Can Learn from Wegmans," *Chronicle of Higher Education,* July 24, 2016.

24. Cone Communications, *2013 Cone Communications Social Impact Study* (2013), http://www.conecomm.com/research-blog/2013-cone-communications-social-impact-study.

25. Frick, "Millennials Are Cynical Do-Gooders."

26. The calculation, documented time and again, includes lost productivity, recruiting costs, and the opportunity cost of losing an employee who understands the company's

culture. For an example, see Karlyn Borysenko, "What Was Management Thinking? The High Cost of Employee Turnover" (April 22, 2015), eremedia.com/tlnt/what-was-leadership-thinking-the-shockingly-high-cost-of-employee-turnover/.

27. Bentley University, *The PreparedU Project: An In-Depth Look at Millennial Preparedness for Today's Workforce*, https://www.slideshare.net/BentleyU/prepared-u-project-on-millennial-preparedness.

28. Bentley University, "PreparedU: The Millennial Mind Goes to Work," *in SlideShare* (November 11, 2014), https://www.slideshare.net/BentleyU/preparedu-the-millennial-mind-goes-to-work-41415813.

29. National Center for Education Statistics, Table 302.10, "Recent High School Completers and Their Enrollment in 2-Year and 4-Year Colleges, by Sex: 1960 through 2013," *Digest of Education Statistics* (July 2014), https://nces.ed.gov/programs/digest/d14/tables/dt14_302.10.asp.

30. US Census Bureau, "CPS October 2015—Detailed Tables: Table 5. Type of College and Year Enrolled for College Students 15 Years and Over, by Age, Sex, Race, Attendance Status, Control of School, and Enrollment Status: October 2015," https://www.census.gov/data/tables/2015/demo/school-enrollment/2015-cps.html.

31. National Center for Education Statistics, "Fast Facts" (2017), Tables 322.40 and 322.50, https://nces.ed.gov/fastfacts/display.asp?id=37.

32. Julie Coffman and Bill Nuenfeldt, *Everyday Moments of Truth; Frontline Managers Are Key to Women's Career Aspirations,* Bain & Company (June 17, 2014), http://www.bain.com/publications/articles/everyday-moments-of-truth.aspx.

33. Ibid. The report cites one study showing that companies with highly engaged employees grow as much as 2.5 times faster than those with low engagement.

34. Christine Silva, Nancy M. Carter, and Anna Beninger, *Good Intentions, Imperfect Execution? Women Get Fewer of the "Hot Jobs" Needed to Advance,* Catalyst (2012), http://www.catalyst.org/knowledge/good-intentions-imperfect-execution-women-get-fewer-hot-jobs-needed-advance. According to the report, 70 percent of development happens on the job; 20 percent is attributed to networking, mentoring, and sponsorship; only 10 percent happens in formal development programs.

35. Andrea S. Kramer and Alton B. Harris, "Are U.S. Millennial Men Just as Sexist as Their Dads?" *Harvard Business Review,* June 15, 2016, https://hbr.org/2016/06/are-u-s-millennial-men-just-as-sexist-as-their-dads.

Afterword

1. Alex Granados, "What It Was Like to Take the 1917 CPA Exam," *Journal of Accountancy,* June 20, 2016, http://www.journalofaccountancy.com/newsletters/2016/jun/1917-cpa-exam.html.

2. Gene Smiley, "The U.S. Economy in the 1920s," Economic History Association. https://eh.net/encyclopedia/the-u-s-economy-in-the-1920s/.

NAME INDEX

SUBJECT INDEX

A

Academic leadership: higher education's focus on developing, 22–23; how campus experience helps to develop, 115; national and global vested interest in, 24; research and discovery form of, 23; the residential experience to develop personal and, 105–107

Academic projects: experiential learning provided through long-term, 87–88; as key undergraduate factor for college and post-college success, 10, 73

AdmitSee.com, 100

Advertisement: cost-per-thousand (CPM) pricing or "eyeballs" model of, 52; Google's "click-through" model replacing CPM model, 52–53

Afghanistan War, 181

Airbnb, 190

Alamo Community Colleges (San Antonio), 4, 34, 44

Alumni: Gallup-Purdue Index (2014) on career services and donations by, 121; Gallup-Purdue report on success factors for, 9–10

Amazon: Amazon web hosting (AWS), 54; creating business opportunities, 53, 54; crowd wisdom of the star ratings of, 190

American Colleges and Universities (AACU), 45

American University, 1

Americans with Disabilities Act, 178

AmeriCorps, 110

Antioch College (Ohio), 24–25, 140

Apple: creatively teaming iPod with ITunes store, 54; left-brain/right-brain attributes of the best at, 53, 57–58; today's students growing up with, 190

Aspen Institute, 16

AT&T, 50

Atlanta Journal-Constitution, 169

Authenticity, 15

Authority: developmental change in response to, 105; Generation X's attitude toward, 172; student observation of how professors' wear their, 110–111; support to students from, 73; today's students and their attitude toward, 176–177

B

Babson College, 145

Baby Boomers: comparing them to other generations, 175–177, 181; comparing today's students with, 172–174; impact on the workplace by, 62; working side-by-side with other generations, 57–64, 173–174

Bain & Company, 200–201

Bank of America, 5

Barnes & Noble, 54

Bates College, 112

Being Mortal (Gawande), 137

BELL (Business, Entrepreneurship, and Liberal Learning) project [Carnegie Foundation], 136